Writing Clearly

Responding to ESL Compositions

by

Linda Bates, Janet Lane, and Ellen Lange
University of California, Davis

HEINLE & HEINLE PUBLISHERS

A Division of Wadsworth, Inc.
Boston, Massachusetts 02116

Heinle & Heinle Publishers is a division of Wadsworth, Inc.

Manufactured in the United States of America.

ISBN 08384-42072

10 9 8 7 6 5 4 3 2 1

CONTENTS

Preface

Writing Clearly: Responding to ESL Compositions offers instructors an overall system for responding to their ESL students' writing. It includes the following information that is essential for responding effectively to ESL writing:

- how to respond as collaborator and as constructive critic

- how to respond to content in an ESL paper

- how to respond to sentences in an ESL paper

- how to assign grades to an ESL paper

- how to help ESL students benefit from the instructor's feedback on content and sentences

- how to design grading standards

For responding to sentences, the text provides instructors with an effective and efficient system, including a set of 15 grading symbols that can be used to respond to sentence errors accurately, clearly, consistently, and selectively. These grading symbols correlate with the 15 units in the companion student text, *Writing Clearly: An Editing Guide.*

This system for responding to ESL students' writing helps ESL students improve their language control and encourages them to develop strategies for avoiding sentence-level errors in their writing. It is highly recommended that instructors who use the grading symbols and error analysis system in this book also have their students use *Writing Clearly: An Editing Guide.*

Acknowledgments

We are grateful to the Undergraduate Instructional Improvement Program of the Teaching Resources Center at the University of California, Davis, for partially funding an earlier, much smaller version of this material, *Resource Manual for Responding to ESL Compositions,* written for the UC Davis Composition Program. During its writing, we received help from many different people. We greatly appreciate the guidance we received from Laura Stokes, especially her great patience in reading and giving suggestions on multiple drafts of the manuscript. We also thank John Boe for reading and commenting on the final draft of the manuscript. In addition, the comments of our two outside readers, Melinda Erickson and June McKay, helped us make changes that strengthened the text. Our special thanks go to Mary Lowry, Gwendolyn T. Schwabe, and Marlene Clarke, who gave so freely of their time in reading and commenting on the text.

During the process of writing this textbook, which evolved from the earlier work, we had the encouragement and guidance of the staff of Heinle & Heinle Publishers, including Erik Gundersen, editor, and Lynn Telson Barsky, associate editor. We are also indebted to Kristin Thalheimer, production editor, for skillfully overseeing the project; to Will Van Dorp, our copy editor, who made many useful suggestions; and to Maryellen Eschmann, who guided the manuscript through the final stages. We are also grateful to the reviewers who made many excellent suggestions on earlier drafts of the text: Olga Aleman, Austin Community College, Texas; Lida Baker, UCLA Extension, Los Angeles, California; June Chatterjee, Department for International Students, Contra Costa College, California; Brian Hickey, English Language Institute, Manhattanville College, Purchase, New York; Kevin Keating, Center for English as a Second Language, University of Arizona, Tucson; Heather Robertson, California State University, Los Angeles, American Culture and Language Program; and Carole Rosen, International English Language Institute, Hunter College, City University of New York.

We are indebted to the following for providing sample grading standards: The University of California, Davis, English for Nonnative Speakers Undergraduate Program, for its English 21, 22, and 23 Grading Standards and Final Exam Grading Standards; and to George Gadda and the University of California President's Office for the Subject A Scoring Guide.

We are also indebted to the following instructors who generously provided sample papers from their ESL classes: Marjorie Baertschi of the University of California, Davis, Extension Intensive English Program; Suzanne Pope-Mathews of the University of California, Davis, Linguistics Program; and Lisa Marchand of Cosumnes River College, Sacramento. Most importantly, we are indebted to the great number of ESL students who contributed their sentences, paragraphs, and essays as examples for this textbook. Without their generosity, this book would not have been possible.

PART 1:

How the Instructor Can Respond
to ESL Compositions

■ CHAPTER 1:   Introduction

This text, *Writing Clearly: Responding to ESL Compositions,* and the student book, *Writing Clearly: An Editing Guide,* work together as companion texts that will help you as a busy instructor respond effectively and efficiently to the content and sentences of ESL compositions, while also providing your ESL students with an easy system for using the sentence-level feedback you give them by marking their compositions.

The Teacher Sourcebook

In this text, *Writing Clearly: Responding to ESL Compositions,* you will learn ways to respond to ESL compositions that will make your response to content, response to sentences, and determination of grades efficient for you and effective for students in terms of helping them improve their writing.

You will learn:

- how to respond to content in ESL papers

- how to respond to sentences in ESL papers

- how to put together response to content, response to sentences, and a grade in an end comment

- how to help your students implement a systematic approach to error analysis, using the feedback you give them on sentence errors

This method of responding to ESL compositions is presented in a step-by-step, user-friendly approach. Each step is first presented briefly "in a nutshell" so that you can implement this system quickly. Fuller explanations of theory and background are also included (and clearly designated as such) so that as time permits, those who want to read more about theory can do so.

You will also find particularly helpful the sample student papers in Chapter 5, where you will see examples of different ways instructors can respond to various types of ESL papers. You will also find valuable the reference section at the end of *Writing Clearly: Responding to ESL Compositions* ("Works Cited" and "Categorized Bibliography"), which will refer you to additional reading on responding to compositions, error analysis, language acquisition, the monitor theory, and faculty response to ESL errors.

The Student Text

Your students will find *Writing Clearly: An Editing Guide* a user-friendly text that not only makes ESL students aware of common ESL language problems in writing but also gives the students strategies for correcting and reducing these errors. The book guides students through 15 common ESL errors with a combination of explanations, rules, and self-help strategies, along with exercises for practice that move students from correcting errors in practice exercises to correcting them in their own writing. At the end of each unit, students have the opportunity to plan, write, and revise a writing assignment in order to practice what they have learned in the unit.

How the Student Text Can Be Used

The student text has great flexibility in that it can be used in several different teaching situations:

1. **As a course on its own** in improving language control in the context of writing.

   The student textbook can be used as the sole text for a course in improving language control in writing. In this case, you will most likely have the students do the writing assignments at the end of each unit.

2. **As a component of a writing course** where students are doing writing assignments outside of this textbook.

   The student textbook can be used effectively along with a separate composition book and/or reader. In this case, you may or may not choose to have students do the writing assignments at the end of each unit.

3. **As supplementary material** for ESL writers enrolled in a composition course geared towards native speakers of English, such as a freshman college writing course or a technical writing course for engineers.

   In this case, you can use the grading symbols when marking an ESL student's paper. You can ask the student to purchase *Writing Clearly: An Editing Guide* and to set priorities for working on errors. The student can then work individually, using the explanations and exercises in the units.

Why It Is Important to Use the Teacher Sourcebook with the Student Book

This teacher sourcebook differs from the standard instructor's manual because it offers you a complete system for responding to the content and sentences in

ESL students' writing. For responding to sentences, it provides an effective and efficient system, including a set of 15 grading symbols that can be used to respond to sentence errors *accurately, clearly, consistently,* and *selectively.* These grading symbols correlate with the 15 units in the student book.

While you can use the student book alone, simply adopting the 15 grading symbols to mark papers, this approach to sentence-level marking is not necessarily the most beneficial method of helping ESL students improve their writing. Instead, you will find it more beneficial for the student if you respond to sentences within the greater context of responding to content, as well as within the context of student analysis of errors, both of which are explained in practical and theoretical terms *only* in the teacher sourcebook. In addition, if you simply adopted the 15 grading symbols in the student book, you would not benefit from the explanations in the teacher sourcebook of how to use these grading symbols accurately, consistently, clearly, and selectively.

The Instructor Response System

In this chapter, you will find an explanation of your dual roles as a responder to ESL compositions—responder to content and responder to sentences. First, you will find a brief overview of your roles in response to content and to sentences. Next, if you wish to read more about the theory of responding to ESL compositions, you will find, identified with a ▼, a more detailed presentation of the theory and background behind this response system in boxes.

First, read the sections below on the dual roles of the instructor in responding to content and to sentences. You can then read the brief explanation of how teacher response and student error analysis work in tandem, and, if you wish, the background/theory sections of this unit.

The Instructor's Dual Role When Responding to ESL Papers

When responding to an ESL composition, you have a dual role:

- collaborator in response to content
- constructive critic in response to sentence errors

A. Collaborator in Response to Content

In responding to the content of an ESL composition, you will want to do the following:

1. **Respond as an interested, engaged reader.** In the first role as collaborator, you ideally function as an interested reader, not a judge, hunter of errors, or appropriator of the student's text. As an engaged reader, you can also help the student see not only the strengths of a piece of writing but also the weaknesses that need attention during revision. In this role, you reinforce the idea that writing is a process, not a product.

2. **Make positive comments in order to motivate the student and to balance negative comments.** As collaborator, you need to keep in mind that one of your most important roles is that of a motivator. By providing motivating comments, you can encourage the student to continue writing and to take risks in writing instead of focusing only on errors or being afraid to write for fear of making errors.

▼ **Background:** This positive "affective" feedback (that is, feedback within the domain of feelings and emotions) can be very important because, as research shows, within this positive affective climate, the student can more easily receive negative messages (Beavens 1977; Cardelle and Corno 1981; Krashen 1982), whether the negative feedback is in response to content or language.

Thus you will always want to keep in mind the importance of your role as collaborator in response to content. (In Chapter 2, you will find practical approaches to responding to content. In Chapter 4, you will find guidance on how to balance response to content with response to sentence-level errors.)

B. Constructive Critic in Response to Sentence Errors

In the second role as constructive critic, you will respond to sentence-level features of the ESL paper. Yet in considering responding to sentences, you may have asked the following question:

Why Do ESL Students Need Response to Sentence Errors?

ESL students need sentence-level feedback because:

1. Sentence-level feedback is an essential part of the process of acquiring a second language.

2. Sentence-level feedback helps students reduce the number of errors in their writing so that they can conform to the high standards of academic and professional writing.

3. Many ESL students desire sentence-level feedback.

1. Sentence-Level Feedback Is an Essential Part of the Process of Acquiring a Second Language

In order to understand the essential nature of feedback in the student's language learning process, you will find helpful the following overview of several linguistic theories (especially if you have not had formal training in linguistics):

- second language acquisition

- interlanguage

- error analysis

Second Language Acquisition

Students move toward proficiency in a second language through a process that involves both *acquisition* (the subconscious incorporation of linguistic forms primarily through reading/listening) and *learning* (the conscious assimilation of rules and forms through individual study or classroom instruction).

FIGURE 1.1:   Attaining Proficiency in a Second Language

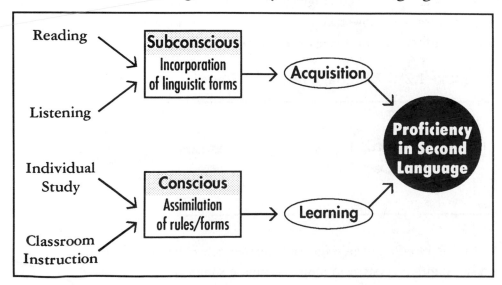

▼ **Note:** While acquisition and learning are both parts of the process of attaining proficiency in a second language, you may find it helpful to know that in some cases ESL students may be primarily language learners or language acquirers. Acquirers have usually been in the United States for a number of years and have learned English by being exposed to it in their everyday life rather than by learning rules formally in school. Learners, on the other hand, have usually come more recently to the United States as, for example, foreign exchange students and have reached their particular level of proficiency through formal classroom instruction in English in their own country or in intensive language programs here, where most often formalized grammar instruction is primarily based on rule learning. (Of course, some students newly arrived in the U.S. become adept at acquiring the second language.) Another group of students has had a very limited exposure to English either through acquisition or learning; these students may be recent immigrants who have had little classroom instruction in English and little time to acquire English in this country or immigrants who have been in the U.S. for quite some time but have remained in their ethnic communities, primarily using their native language, rather than English.

Interlanguage

In mastering a second language through a combination of acquisition and learning, learners move through a developmental stage in which they produce what linguists call *interlanguage* (Selinker 1972).

FIGURE 1.2:   Language Learning Stages

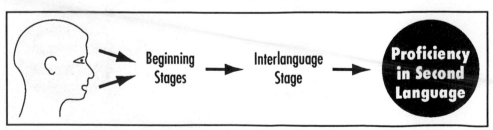

In this interlanguage stage, each learner constructs his or her own idiosyncratic linguistic system in order to impose some sort of order on a seemingly chaotic mass of linguistic forms.

FIGURE 1.3:   Language Learning

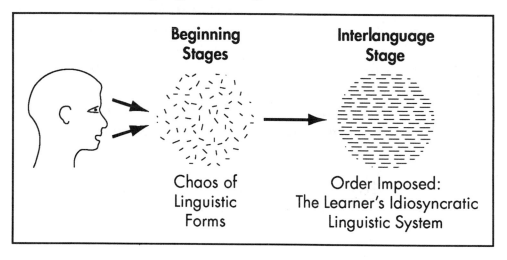

The learner imposes order on the chaos of forms through a trial and error process of *hypothesis formation:*

• the learner forms hypotheses about the structure of the second language

• the learner tests these hypotheses in production (writing/speaking)

• the learner receives feedback from readers or listeners

• the learner modifies these hypotheses based on feedback received.

FIGURE 1.4:   The Trial and Error Process of Hypothesis Formation (with feedback)

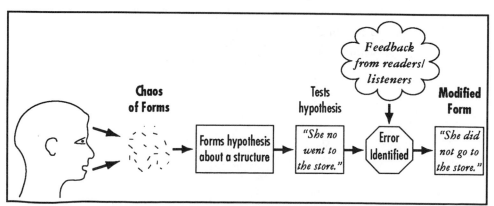

Without appropriate oral or written feedback, the learner will go through this same process, forming hypotheses about the structure of the second language and testing these hypotheses in production. However, without appropriate feedback on an erroneous form, the learner will assume that the hypothesis being tested is correct or that he/she has successfully communicated despite errors. As a result, the incorrect forms (errors) will then become stabilized in the ordered system of language the student is creating; that is, the error becomes *fossilized* in the student's idiosyncratic linguistic system (Vigil and Oller 1976).

FIGURE 1.5:   Trial and Error Process Without Feedback

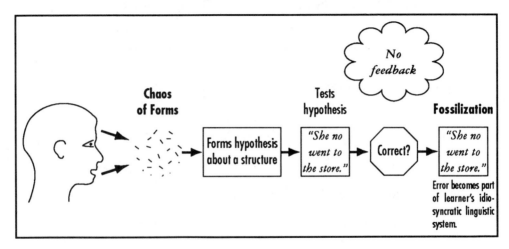

Feedback Prevents Error Fossilization.   As you can see from the previous description of the language learning process, ESL students require feedback in order to avoid fossilization of errors—the process by which incorrect forms become a stabilized part of the learner's idiosyncratic linguistic system. That is, feedback helps *prevent* fossilization of errors.

▼ **Background/Theory:** *Errors are Positive.* Assure your students that errors are, in fact, positive because they indicate that a student is moving forward in the process of developing proficiency in the second language. A number of linguists have discussed the paradoxical concept that errors are positive (Corder 1967; Robb, Ross, and Shortreed 1986; Corder 1981; Brumfit 1980; Lalande 1982; and Horning 1987).

Errors that appear systematically in a student's writing (for example, a repeated error in use of the past perfect) are positive because they indicate that the student is indeed developing his/her own idiosyncratic linguistic system (to order the seeming chaos of language forms in the second language) and is in the process of forming and testing hypotheses about the structure of the second language. Thus the error represents a trial form the student is using to test one of his/her hypotheses about the structure of the language.

Overall, hypothesis testing (and its resulting errors) go hand-in-hand with feedback and error analysis to take the student toward his or her goal of full proficiency in the second language.

Feedback Helps the Learner Overcome Errors Already Fossilized. Feedback can also help the learner identify and begin working on errors that are already fossilized in his or her idiosyncratic language system. For language learners (who may have studied grammatical rules for years), errors may be fossilized because the learner has not received effective feedback on his or her errors in written language. For language acquirers (those ESL students who have picked up English primarily through everyday exposure to the language rather than by formal instruction in school), errors may be fossilized because these students have had little feedback and little opportunity to do error analysis.

Error Analysis: The role of feedback in this text's systematic approach to error analysis.

In order to prevent and overcome errors in ESL students' writing, linguists suggest that students (especially at the high intermediate and advanced stages) use a formal system of error analysis, such as the one presented in this text. This type of systematic approach to error analysis involves the student in conscious study of sentence errors in order to overcome these errors.

Using this text's systematic approach to error analysis, students move through a process that involves a number of steps. It is in the first step of this process (ERROR IDENTIFIED) that feedback plays a critical role.

FIGURE 1.6:   This Text's Systematic Approach to Error Analysis

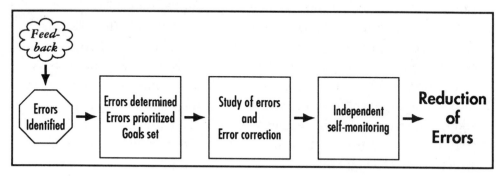

Errors Identified.   Feedback on sentence errors plays an essential role in the first part of the student's error analysis process—*error identification.* Without feedback on errors, most ESL students cannot effectively begin the process of error analysis because they do not know what their sentence errors are. Then, if they do not undertake a conscious and formal system of error analysis, most will not be able to attain the high level of proficiency in the second language that is expected in academic writing; instead, their fossilized errors will remain.

Thus, feedback is an essential part of a systematic approach to error analysis, which in itself is a necessary step in moving toward both fluency and accuracy. Some language learners, of course, may be able to identify and correct their own errors merely by listening to and reading correct models, but most learners need more than this, especially if their errors are fossilized.

▼ **Note:** *Error or Mistake?* As you mark errors in an ESL composition, be aware of the difference between "errors" and "mistakes" so that you will not spend time marking mistakes. In the trial and error process of forming hypotheses about language structures, the learner will necessarily make errors, which are (as noted earlier) positive because they indicate the student is moving forward in the process of developing competency in the second language. Linguists distinguish between these positive errors, which are **systematic** and reflect the learners' developing knowledge of the second language, and mistakes, which are **random** and caused by memory lapses, fatigue, or strong emotions (Corder 1967; Bartholomae 1980; Sridhar 1980; Horning 1987). Mistakes occur **sporadically,** while errors will reoccur **systematically.** For example, one student might make one or two mistakes in subject–verb agreement ("He study") in a composition; another student, however, might have problems with subject–verb agreement in many instances throughout a composition, a problem that is thus systematic and represents an error. Mistakes can easily be self-corrected by the student if he or she is given time to proofread; however, most learners cannot readily correct errors without feedback.

The whole process of error analysis should, ideally, be a *discovery process* for the student. As you will see in later chapters, the instructor's feedback on sentence error is just the first part of this error analysis process, as you will see again in the figure below. The heart of error analysis for the student will be a discovery process in which the student (with some assistance) takes primary responsibility for studying, correcting, and eventually reducing errors.

FIGURE 1.7:   This Text's Systematic Approach to Error Analysis

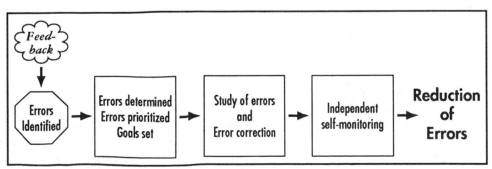

The Goal of Sentence Feedback and Student Error Analysis = Independent Self-Monitoring.   As you provide feedback by marking errors with symbols and assist the student in undertaking the rest of this systematic approach to error analysis, you and the student should keep in mind that the goal for the student is *independent self-monitoring.* In other words, as a result of this systematic approach to error analysis, individual study, and classroom instruction, the student will add to and modify the idiosyncratic linguistic system he or she has been creating so that it will eventually consist of a pool of correct linguistic rules and forms to call upon in order to *self-monitor* the language he or she produces when writing (or speaking). This monitoring might happen pre- or post-production. Instead of depending on feedback from others, the language learner will eventually function as an independent self-monitor, capable of modifying the language he or she produces (Krashen 1982).

FIGURE 1.8:   The Self-Monitor

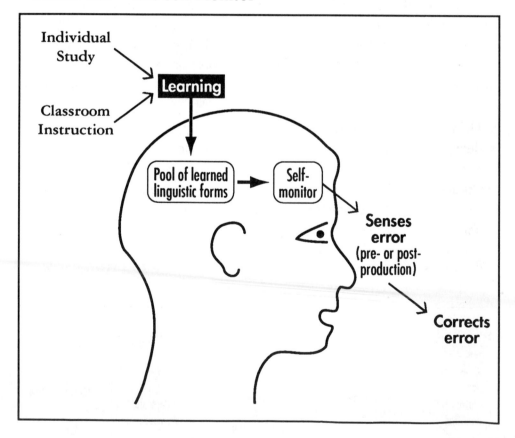

(You will learn more about ways to help your students develop effective self-monitoring strategies in Chapter 6.)

2. Sentence-Level Feedback Helps Students Conform to the High Standards of Academic and Professional Writing

In addition to being an essential part of the learner's language acquisition process, feedback on sentence errors is also important for ESL students because writers of formal written English are held to high standards in both the academic and professional worlds, much higher than the standards of informal spoken English. Readers in both academic and professional settings are highly aware of the standards of formal written English and expect writers to adhere to these standards.

▼ **Background/Theory:** Research has shown that faculty members across the curriculum are not only aware of errors in nonnative English speakers' writing but that they also intuitively rank these errors according to the degree to which the errors interfere with comprehension, rating those errors that impede understanding as the most serious (Vann 1984; Santos 1988). One study of faculty across the curriculum (Santos 1988) showed that while faculty generally consider content as the most important part of a paper, they also evaluate the language of these papers, judging ESL errors as "academically unacceptable" and ranking those errors that interfere with the meaning of a paper as the most serious. Another study showed that faculty across the curriculum rate ESL errors as the least acceptable type of sentence-level errors in a paper, as opposed to the types of errors native speakers make, such as spelling, punctuation, pronoun agreement (Vann 1984).

In his study of error in compositions of ESL students and native speakers, McGirt found that English composition instructors will tolerate slightly more errors in an ESL writer's composition than a native speaker's; however, their threshold for tolerating ESL errors is not very high— 3 errors/100 words in the ESL paper versus 1 error/100 words in the native speaker paper (McGirt 1984, cited in Celce-Murcia 1988).

---

3. Many ESL Students Desire Sentence-Level Feedback

Feedback is also important because, as surveys show, many ESL students desire feedback on their sentence errors because they realize that in formal academic discourse, sentence-level accuracy does count.

▼ **Background/Theory:** For more on what surveys show about student preferences for sentence-level feedback, see Leki 1986.

What Kind of Feedback on Sentence Errors Do ESL Students Need?

To be successful at error analysis and thus move toward both fluency and accuracy, ESL students need sentence-level feedback that is *accurate, clear, consistent,* and *selective.* These are the principles underlying the marking system you will learn more about in Chapter 3.

▼ **Background/Theory:** Numerous researchers have suggested that to be beneficial, feedback on errors must be accurate, clear, consistent, and selective, that is, priority given to those errors that most interfere with communication (Cohen and Robbins 1976; Dulay and Burt 1977; Hendrickson 1980; Lalande 1982; Walz 1982; Horning 1987). Research has also shown that this type of feedback leads to improved performance (Cardelle and Corno 1981; Lalande 1982; Fathman and Whalley 1985 & 1990) and that the majority of ESL students do attend to this type of feedback on written compositions (Cohen 1987; Radecki and Swales 1988).

How Does Instructor Response to Errors Work in Tandem with Student Error Analysis?

Feedback on sentence errors works best when it is incorporated into a systematic approach to error analysis, such as the one you will learn more about in Chapters 3 and 6. While this error analysis process will involve the instructor or a tutor in identifying the student's errors, especially initially, it should be set up largely as a discovery process for the student, one in which students assume some or even much of the responsibility for error analysis. They are then far more likely to be motivated and to progress rapidly in becoming independent self-monitors. As noted earlier, an important goal of this process is to help the student eventually become a self-editor, capable of revising his or her text for both content and sentence-level features.

▼ **Background/Theory:** Several researchers have suggested practical approaches to error analysis (Hendrickson 1980a; Lalande 1982; Walz 1982; Raimes 1991). Researchers have also suggested that teachers need to ensure that their students are using a discovery process (Corder 1967; Hendrickson 1980) in which the student (with help from the teacher or a tutor at the early stages) takes a major part of the responsibility for analyzing errors and eventually moves to "self-monitoring," where the student independently discovers and corrects errors.

■ CHAPTER 2: Responding to Content

As you read in Chapter 1, one of your roles in responding to a student's paper is to give the student feedback on content. In this role, you are an interested reader, a motivator who encourages the student to continue writing and a coach who guides the student in improving his or her writing.

This chapter is organized around four questions instructors frequently have about responding to the content of a student's paper. You will first find the answers to these questions. You will then sometimes find background/theory sections or notes which you may choose to read if time permits. These sections (marked ▼) give you more detail about research or elaborate on options you have in terms of responding to content. At the end of the chapter, you will find a student's paper with an instructor's response to content.

Although instructors' responses to student papers usually contain feedback on both content and language, the explanations and sample instructor responses in this chapter focus exclusively on response to content. In Chapter 4, you will find suggestions for combining response to content and sentence-level features in an end comment. Then in Chapter 5, there are sample papers that illustrate instructors' responses to both content and language.

In this chapter, you will find answers to the following four questions:

Question 1: *Why Is It Important to Respond to Content?*

Question 2: *How Can You Effectively Respond to Content?*

Question 3: *Where on the Paper Should You Respond to Content?*

Question 4: *When in the Writing Process Should You Give Feedback on Content?*

Question 1: Why Is It Important to Respond to Content?

In an ESL paper, the ESL sentence-level errors are often the most noticeable feature. Nevertheless, in addition to responding to the sentence-level errors, it is equally important that you respond to the content of an ESL paper for the following reasons:

A. Feedback on content often helps improve content in subsequent drafts and future papers.

B. Feedback on content is desired by the majority of ESL writers.

C. Feedback on content gives ESL writers feedback they may need on thinking and organizational patterns they have transferred from their native language to English.

D. Feedback on content can help the student develop a sense of audience.

A. Feedback on content often helps improve the content of subsequent drafts and future papers.

As a busy instructor, you may wonder whether you should spend valuable time responding to content. Does response to content improve the content of subsequent drafts and future papers? Although some reviews of research on native speaker and ESL writers seem to suggest that response to content has little effect on performance (Hillocks 1986; Leki 1990), a recent study on ESL writers (Fathman and Whalley 1990) has shown that feedback on content can, indeed, help improve the content of subsequent drafts.

Although very little research has been done on how well response to content on one paper transfers to future papers a student writes, at least one study on native speakers (Schroeder 1973, cited in Fathman and Whalley 1990) suggests that positive feedback on content does have a positive effect on content in subsequent papers. Furthermore, experienced ESL composition instructors find that when ESL students read the instructor's comments on final drafts, they are often able to make good use of both positive and negative comments to improve the content in subsequent papers. For example, if a student receives feedback indicating that a lack of supporting evidence made his or her paper less convincing than it could have been, the student is likely at least to attempt to provide supporting evidence in subsequent papers because the student's awareness of the importance of this supporting evidence has been heightened. In addition, if a student receives positive feedback on his or her use of interesting specific details, the student is likely to continue using specific details in subsequent writing because the value of using these details has been pointed out.

▼ **Background/Theory:** Many questions remain unanswered regarding students' processing of teachers' response. For example, Leki (1990) raises the questions of whether or not students read the feedback and whether or not they understand the feedback if they read it. Similarly, Cohen and Cavalcanti (1990) point out that composition researchers have questioned whether students' main concern is the grade on a paper (leading them to not read the instructors' comments carefully) and whether students are limited in their strategies for revising even if they do read the instructor's comments. These questions suggest that researchers believe, as many experienced composition instructors do, that response to content is, in fact, useful if students read it, understand it, and are given guidance on strategies for revision.

Fathman and Whalley's study (1990) on ESL writers gives concrete evidence that response to content does, in fact, improve content in subsequent drafts. Although they found improvement in the content of subsequent drafts even without teacher response to content, the content of subsequent drafts improved much more when teacher response to content was given. Fathman and Whalley also found that feedback on content positively affected subsequent drafts whether content feedback alone was given or whether feedback on content was given along with feedback on sentence-level features.

B. The majority of ESL writers desire feedback on content.

Recent studies on ESL writers (Radecki and Swales 1988; Cohen and Cavalcanti 1990) have found that the majority of ESL writers desire feedback on content. Experienced composition instructors also report that a great majority of their students ask for and appreciate feedback on content.

▼ **Background/Theory:** Although a few studies done on native speakers have indicated that some students may either feel negatively toward or disinterested in feedback on content, this research is as yet inconclusive and may not be directly applicable to ESL writers' response to content feedback. See Leki (1986), who, in a review of research on responding, discusses several studies on student reactions to feedback on content.

C. ESL writers may need feedback on thinking and organizational patterns they have transferred from their native language to English.

ESL students may particularly need feedback on content because they may be using thinking and organizational patterns that they have transferred from their native language and which are not used in English writing. Native speakers of many Asian languages, for example, may not state their points clearly in English because when writing in their native language they are expected not to state their point directly but rather to go around it indirectly, a thinking and writing style common in Asian languages but confusing and vague to an English-speaking reader. Likewise, native speakers of many Romance languages, such as Spanish and Portuguese, may veer off the topic when writing in English because when writing in their native language they have much more freedom to digress from the topic than an English-speaking writer has. Yet these digressions give an English-speaking reader the impression that a piece of writing is disorganized. Thus, in responding to content, you can point out to the student these important rhetorical differences by telling the student, for example, to state the point directly or to avoid veering off the topic.

▼ **Background/Theory:** Instructors do not need knowledge of the thinking and organizational patterns common in a student's native language in order to recognize rhetorical patterns that are not effective in English. However, instructors who are interested in this area may want to refer to the research on contrastive rhetoric. The following are some valuable sources of information: Beebe 1988; Connor and Kaplan 1987; Gregg 1986; Koreo 1988; Meyers 1985; Reid 1992.

D. Feedback on content can help the student develop a sense of audience.

By responding to content, you can also help the student develop a sense of audience. By responding as an interested reader, you help the writer become aware of the needs of his or her audience. For example, as an engaged reader responding to content, you can indicate areas in a paper where the reader would be helped by having more information about a particular point. In addition, you can point out areas that, as an interested reader, you particularly liked. These kinds of comments ultimately help heighten the student's awareness of the needs of his or her audience. This sense of audience can eventually be internalized, leading the writer to become much more capable of revising his or her own writing independently rather than depending solely on the instructor's feedback.

Question 2: How Can You Effectively Respond to Content?

In order to respond effectively to the content of a student's paper, you will find the following four suggestions helpful. Then at the end of this section, you will find a student writing sample with an instructor's response that incorporates these four suggestions.

- A. Write personalized comments.
- B. Provide guidance or direction when necessary.
- C. Make text-specific comments.
- D. Balance positive and negative comments.

A. Write personalized comments.

As discussed earlier in this chapter, you will want to respond to a paper as an interested reader who is engaged in the text. One way to do this is to write personalized comments, that is, comments that reflect your personal reaction or response to the ideas in a student's paper. As an interested reader, you will want to respond to the text in a warm, human voice, commenting on elements in the text that are particularly appealing, yet not neglecting those parts of the text that are unclear or need strengthening. Such comments not only encourage the student to continue writing but also contribute to the student's development of a sense of audience discussed in the previous section of this chapter.

B. Provide guidance or direction when necessary.

One of the considerations in responding to a text is, of course, how much input you can give the student without taking control of the student's text. Although you do not want to completely appropriate a text, providing guidance or direction may be necessary, especially for ESL students who may be inexperienced in academic writing in English or may lack knowledge of the rhetorical structures of English. For example, you may need to suggest that a student analyze a point further or support a point with specific details. Or you may need to make suggestions on how to strengthen organization.

C. Make text-specific comments.

In formulating comments, you should consider how specific you want to make your comments. Research shows that text-specific comments are immensely helpful to the student (Sommers 1982; Zamel 1985). In a text-specific comment, you might say, "I liked the example about your sister." In a general comment, on the other hand, you might say, "Good example," a comment you could apply to any example in any paper. Although ideally text-specific comments are best, some research on ESL writers shows that even general comments help writers improve the content of subsequent drafts (Fathman and Whalley 1990).

D. Balance positive and negative comments.

In your role as motivator and collaborator, it is important to balance positive and negative feedback. As discussed in Chapter 1, positive comments allow you first to establish a "positive affective climate" (Beavens 1977; Cardelle and Corno 1981; Krashen 1982) so that a student can more easily receive the negative feedback on content (and sentence-level features) that you may need to give.

Sample Response To Content

What follows is a student response (written in class) to a short-answer essay question. The end comment illustrates the four suggestions for responding effectively to content discussed in this section. The comments are *personalized* and *text-specific.* They also show *a positive and negative balance* and *provide guidance and direction* to the student on the need for a stronger initial focus on the question being answered.

Writing Topic:

Discuss the progress you have made so far on your term paper assignment for this class. In addition to explaining what you have already done and what you are currently working on, comment on the aspect of writing a term paper that has been most challenging for you.

Student Response:

My progress in English has been great. Today, I feel more confident in my work and I think I have learned a lot.

I had worked in different aspects of the English language such as reading, conversation, listening and comprehension, grammar and writing.

I am currently working on my term paper, collecting the information, organizing it, and trying to get the table of contents. I almost have all the papers that I am going to include in this paper. I started to read some of them and take notes on the main ideas.

I think that the most challenging part for me will be to paraphrase and summarize all the information and get the conclusions.

End Comment:

I am glad you are progressing well on your term paper. I certainly agree that learning how to summarize and paraphrase effectively in a new language is challenging.

When responding to short-answer essay questions, you will want to focus immediately on the question. Your response was somewhat confusing at the beginning because you did not directly answer the question until the third paragraph. Yet once you did focus on the question, you were careful to answer both parts of it—good work!

Question 3: Where on the Paper Should You Respond to Content?

Whether you are responding to early drafts or final drafts, you have several options in terms of where on the paper to put response to content. You can respond:

A. In the margins

B. In an end comment

C. Both in the margins and in an end comment

However, whichever of these options you choose, you should remember:

    D. **Avoid overwhelming the student with too many comments.**

A. Responding in the margins

You may find it useful to make marginal comments to the student as you are reading, especially on long papers. These marginal comments can be especially helpful because they signal to the student the exact location of a problem area (such as an unclear point, an organizational problem, or a lack of specifics) or an area that is especially well written.

    Yet in order to avoid the student's feeling overwhelmed by seeing too many comments written all over the paper, you may want to restrict your comments to one side of the paper, either the left margin or the right margin.

▼ **Note:** Some instructors find that they like to respond to content by writing a comment at the end of a paragraph. If you choose to do this, make sure that it is clear to the student that you are responding to the previous, rather than the subsequent, paragraph. You can often clarify what you are doing by telling students in class or in conference how to interpret a comment located at the end of a paragraph.

B. Responding in an end comment

You may prefer not to write in the margins of a student's paper. Perhaps you feel that responding in the margins as you are reading a paper interrupts your concentration, making it difficult for you to judge the overall effectiveness of the paper. For this reason or other reasons, you may choose to wait to respond until you reach the end of the paper, thus putting all your comments on content in an end comment.

C. Responding both in the margins and in an end comment

You may choose, as many instructors do, to select both of the above options and respond both in the margins and in an end comment. If you choose this method, you should tailor your end comment to reflect what you have pointed out in any marginal comments.

D. Avoiding an overwhelming number of comments

You will want to avoid overwhelming the student with too many comments, whether in the margins, at the end of the paper, or in both places. An overwhelming number of comments may not only discourage the student but also may lead to the student's being overly dependent on your feedback, thus preventing the student from developing the skills needed to read his or her own writing critically and to progress as a writer.

Question 4: When in the Writing Process Should You Give Feedback on Content?

As discussed previously in this chapter, the research on when during the student's writing process feedback is best given is inconclusive for both native speakers and ESL writers.

▼ **Background/Theory:** In surveying the literature (on both response to content and sentence-level features), Cohen and Cavalcanti (1990) report that writing instructors seem to favor giving feedback to students during the writing process (that is on early and later drafts of papers), whereas students tend to prefer instructors to respond to the final version of a paper.

Many experienced writing instructors, however, find that their students greatly appreciate feedback on drafts as well as final papers.

Given the lack of consensus on when in the writing process to respond to content, you have several options. You can choose to respond to one or a combination of the following:

A. To early drafts

B. To later drafts

C. To the final draft

A. Responding to early drafts

Depending upon the demands of the assignment, the student's needs, and your own time constraints, you may choose to respond to content on early drafts of an assignment. You may want to do this to check early on in a student's writing process whether or not the student has approached a topic effectively and to give guidance if he or she has not. Conversely, you may prefer not to respond to the student's earliest drafts and instead to give him or her more responsibility for revising early drafts. If you choose not to respond to early drafts, you may find it useful to have students respond to each other's drafts in peer response groups before you look at later or final drafts.

B. Responding to later drafts

Another option you have is to respond to later drafts of a student's paper, material the student may have already revised on his or her own or with the input of classmates or a tutor. You may feel, as mentioned above, that by allowing the student to work on the initial drafts on his or her own, you are giving the student more responsibility for revising. You may also feel that you would rather respond to drafts that are better in quality than the very earliest drafts. The major advantage of responding to later drafts is that doing so gives you a chance to indicate to a student before a paper is submitted for a grade some of the areas in which a paper is particularly effective in terms of content or areas which need work in order to make the paper more effective.

C. Responding to the final draft

Another option you have is to respond to content only on a student's final draft. Many experienced ESL instructors, especially those with heavy teaching loads, choose this option, although they often elect to use peer response groups for response to drafts. If you do choose this option, to respond only to the final draft, you will still want to emphasize to the student the value of doing drafts, whether or not you collect and/or give credit for them. The content of students' papers will most likely improve when they do multiple drafts of papers, even if you do not respond to these drafts.

▼ **Background/Theory:** A recent study on ESL writers (Cohen and Cavalcanti 1990) showed that the content of students' papers improved on subsequent drafts even when no instructor feedback on content was given on drafts.

Student Paper Illustrating Response to Content

The paper that follows was written by a student in an intermediate ESL writing course at the university level. The paper was written in the classroom during a two-hour class period after the students had read and discussed an article on the amount of time American children spend watching television and the types of programs they watch. The writer of this paper was required to revise the paper and submit it later in the term as an out-of-class essay assignment. For the purposes of this book, since grading standards differ from program to program, the paper has not been given a grade. It also does not contain any response to sentence-level features since the focus of this chapter is response to content.

The teacher response illustrates many of the principles of responding to content that have been discussed in this chapter. You will note that the paper has both marginal comments as well as an end comment.

Writing topic:

What are the effects on American children of their watching four hours per day of television?

Student Response:

Television, what will life be if there's no television on this world? Anybody can get bore to death at home without television, but what if a person watch too much television? He would not be as clever as a friend at his age. Especially the children, too much television could affect them many ways such as becoming activeless, and getting behind on everything. Out of those affects, the two most significant affects of American children watching almost four hours of television each day are learning the violences on television and slowing down their learning abilities. | *Good focus on the question here.*

Watching to much television gives the American children a greater chance immitating the violences on television. Many today's | *Good point.*

American children watch television immediate at the time they come back from school. After the cartoon's program is over, they start to do their homework. That is the great idea but they continue to watch other programs after cartoon. That's the problem. Some programs contain adult languages. The children would learn the language at the first time when they hear the words. Later on, they will say the same stuff over to any person if they think the situation is the same as on television. Besides, television is the program that play people's imaginary or react what one has done including bad and good things. The childrens are like a monkey. They copy everything they see. For example. A child sees a boy in the movie steals his mother's money to buy candy. What if the child's mother doesn't give him the money? The next step the child would do is stepping into his mother's room and steal her purse. Moreover, there's more than stealing money in the movie. In some cases, one person kills another because a tiny problem. Even though it's not real but the child can't distint between reality in life and imaginary in the movie. That is the point that affects the American children of watching too much television.

Is this point related to violence?

Could you make this point clearer?

Does this example relate to violence?

Good here. Could you develop this point (which is on violence)?

Besides immitating television's violences, watching to much television would lead the American children getting behind their friends. Many today's parents let their children joining sports after coming home school avoiding weakness on their children, but some kids rather stay home watching all their favorite program instead of go-

Could you make the effect clearer here?

ing out and playing even though they like playing with their friends too. Because of loving watching television too much, the children don't even care of anything. From this, they have no choice <u>to learn anything that their friends learn.</u> They have no chance to experience anything. For example, Mr. Lee's child does all sort of thing such as climb trees, play baseball in spring, go skiing in the winter and do anything the child wants. As the same time, Mr. Kim's child doesn't step out of the door. He only watch television instead of going out. When the two children meet, Mr. Kim's child would get behind Mr. Lee's child. This hurt Mr. Kim's child from physical to emotional. Therefore, watching too much television could bring the child down.

Learning finally comes up here.

Good specific example about the two children.

How is Mr. Kim's child behind?

It's nothing with watching television but watch too much television could affect a person at any age. It brings a person to dull stage. Importantly the children, too much television reduces the children's abilities. To avoid any future problem in the American children, their parents should limited their time in watching television to one hour a day and the rest of the time let them do other activities.

Good suggestion.

End Comment:

Your paper is well organized, with a clear focus on the question in your introduction. I particularly liked your comparisons of Mr. Lee's and Mr. Kim's children! Also, your suggestion to limit children's TV watching is a good solution to the problem.

The two effects you have chosen to write about are also good. But the first effect, on violence, is not actually focused on until the last few sentences of the paragraph. The second effect, the effect on learning, needs to be clearer in the topic sentence. You could also improve that paragraph by including more analysis on how TV watching affects learning.

When you revise this paper, you will want to work on making your main point clear at the beginning of the paragraph and then making sure you stay focused on this point throughout the paragraph. Please feel free to see me if you have questions about my comments.

■ CHAPTER 3:   Responding Systematically to Sentence-Level Errors

Along with responding to content, the instructor needs to remember that students also need feedback on ESL sentence-level errors.

In this chapter, you will learn how to respond efficiently and effectively to sentence-level errors. Once you make your choices about marking errors and learn the marking system below, you will find that you can mark ESL sentence errors quickly and efficiently. In addition, you will find that this type of standardized marking system will help your students implement this text's systematic approach to error analysis and thus move toward reduction of errors. In the sections below, you will first see the steps you can take in marking sentence errors. If time permits, you may choose to read the theory/background sections, which give more detail about research on marking sentence-level errors.

In Chapter 6 of this text, you will see: 1) how to make your sentence marking system work hand in hand with helping your students learn to do error analysis, and 2) how your marking system fits with the student book, *Writing Clearly: An Editing Guide*.

In the sections below, you will learn about the following steps in marking sentences:

> **Step 1:** *Be Selective in Marking Errors*
> **Step 2:** *Decide How You Will Mark Errors*
> **Step 3:** *Decide When You Will Mark Errors*
> **Step 4:** *Decide If Others Will Also Identify or Mark Errors*

Step 1:   Be Selective in Marking Errors

Since marking all errors in an ESL paper will overwhelm both the student and the instructor, you will need to be selective in marking errors. In deciding which errors to mark and how many errors overall to mark in a paper, use the following criteria in making your decision:

A. **Give top priority to the most serious errors, those that affect comprehensibility of the text.**

B.   Give high priority to errors that occur most frequently.

C.   Consider the individual student's level of proficiency, attitude, and goals.

D.   Consider marking errors recently covered in class.

A. Give top priority to the most serious errors, those that affect comprehension of the text.

In marking errors, give the highest priority to sentence errors that impede understanding—those that block the reader's understanding of the writer's message. In this system, we call those errors that impede understanding *global errors,* and we call those that do not affect overall comprehensibility *local errors.* Global errors usually involve more than one clause in a text, while local errors are most often isolated errors within a single clause.

▼ **Background on Global/Local Errors:** Linguists such as Burt and Kiparsky have used the global/local distinction. (See Burt and Kiparsky 1972 and Burt 1975). In our ESL error analysis system, we have used the terms **global** and **local** for ESL sentence-level errors in a way that differs slightly from the more technical linguistic use of these terms. For example, we have called all verb tense errors global in order to show that they are among the most serious errors in writing, although a verb tense error affecting only one clause would not be termed global by some linguists. This simplification will help instructors and students readily distinguish between more serious and less serious errors. Had we not simplified the global/local distinction, the number of grading symbols would have been larger and harder for instructors and students to work with.

In the ESL Grading Symbols chart below, you will see ESL sentence errors divided into global and local errors. This division makes it easy for you to give priority to global errors when marking errors. (In the next section, you will learn about ways to use these grading symbols.) In the left hand column, you see the suggested grading symbol; in the middle column, a definition of the error; and in the right hand column, the reference to the page in the student book, *Writing Clearly: An Editing Guide.* Also included under "Other Errors" are ten errors native speakers commonly make that are not included in the system but that the instructor may wish to mark.

ESL Grading Symbols

GLOBAL ERRORS—more serious errors
(These errors usually impede understanding.)

SYMBOL	EXPLANATION	PAGE*
vt	incorrect verb tense	1
vf	verb incorrectly formed	27
modal	incorrect use or formation of a modal	45
cond	incorrect use or formation of a conditional sentence	67
ss	incorrect sentence structure	87
wo	incorrect or awkward word order	109
conn	incorrect or missing connector	127
pass	incorrect formation or use of passive voice	147
unclear	unclear message	163

LOCAL ERRORS—less serious errors
(These errors, while distracting, most often do not impede understanding.)

SYMBOL	EXPLANATION	PAGE*
sv	incorrect subject–verb agreement	169
art	incorrect or missing article	181
num	problem with the singular or plural of a noun	197
wc	wrong word choice, including prepositions	209
wf	wrong word form	221
nonidiom	nonidiomatic (not expressed this way in English)	237

*Note: The pages listed in the right-hand column refer to pages in *Writing Clearly: An Editing Guide,* where a full explanation of each error is given.

OTHER ERRORS
(These errors are commonly made by native speakers.)

SYMBOL	EXPLANATION
cap	capitalization—capital letter needed
coh	coherence—one idea does not lead to the next
cs	comma splice—two independent clauses joined by a comma
dm	dangling modifier—phrase or clause with no word(s) to modify in a sentence
frag	fragment—incomplete sentence
lc	lower case—word(s) incorrectly capitalized
p	punctuation—punctuation incorrect or missing
pro ref pro agree	pronoun reference/agreement—pronoun reference unclear or agreement incorrect
ro	run-on—two independent clauses joined with no punctuation
sp	spelling error—word incorrectly spelled

▼ **Note:** *Why Give Top Priority to Global Errors?* Since global errors make it difficult for the reader to understand the overall meaning of a composition, marking and thus helping the student learn to correct global errors will have the greatest effect on the overall comprehensibility of the student's writing.

For example, the sample sentence below has both global and local errors. Because the global error (the sentence structure problem) makes it difficult for the reader to understand the overall meaning of the sentence, you would want to give it marking priority over the local errors (the number and article problems).

Example: *When we meet new person and start living in totally new environment are scary.*

If you give priority to the local errors and the student corrects only these, the sentence will not be significantly affected, since the global error will still impede understanding.

B. Give high priority to errors that occur most frequently.

Next, decide which global errors to mark since marking all global errors in a paper may overwhelm the student if there are a large number of global errors. In making this decision, consider giving priority to those errors that occur most frequently in a student paper. Some instructors like to glance over the first paragraph or page to make this determination before they begin marking errors. For example, if you see that a student has multiple global errors with verb tense, conditional, sentence structure, and connectors, you may want to draw the student's attention to just those two or three errors that most frequently occur.

▼ **Note:** Of course, if the student has few global errors, but frequent local errors, you may want to give the most frequent local errors priority in marking, since these will be distracting because of their frequency.

C. Consider the individual student's level of proficiency, attitude, and goals.

While the student's most serious and frequent global errors will take top priority, you may also want to consider marking other less serious errors after considering the individual student's level of proficiency, attitude, and goals.

- Consider the student's level of proficiency.

  An advanced student whose text is generally readable and coherent is capable of working on local errors as well as on his or her most serious and frequent global errors, whereas a student at a lower level of proficiency whose text may be incoherent in several places may be able to concentrate only on one or two types of global errors.

- Consider the student's attitude.

  In selecting errors to mark, take into account the student's attitude, including how confident, resistant, or discouraged he or she is. A very confident student will most likely be able to handle receiving feedback on more errors at once than a discouraged or resistant student will.

- Consider the student's goals.

  If you have met with the student in conference, you may know the student's goals and want to consider them when marking sentence errors. For example, you might want to consider whether the student wishes to eliminate the majority of errors or just enough errors to make his or her writing readable.

▼ **Background/Theory:** For more on considering the individual student's concerns when you are marking errors, see Walz 1982.

D. Consider marking errors recently covered in class.

You may also choose to mark errors you have recently covered in classroom instruction. For example, if you have recently covered subject–verb agreement in class, you may choose to mark these errors in student papers, even if they are not the most serious or frequent errors in the paper.

▼ **Note:** Instead of taking the four above criteria into consideration, the instructor can always opt simply to mark global errors alone.

Step 2:   Decide How You Will Mark Errors

Once you have decided which errors and how many to mark, you are ready to begin marking them in a student paper.

In this section you will learn how to use the grading symbols in the ESL Grading Symbol Chart below to implement what researchers suggest is the most effective way of marking errors. (Here you will learn to use only the first 15 ESL grading symbols, not the symbols for native-speaker errors under "Other Errors.") The suggested method of marking errors that follows will allow you to

- locate the error for the student

- identify the located error with a grading symbol

Look once again at the grading symbols in the left-hand column of the Grading Symbols chart. Notice that each type of error has a corresponding abbreviation, brief enough to allow you to mark sentence errors quickly yet clear enough that students, with a little practice, can easily see the error.

As a feature of this set of grading symbols, certain types of verb errors have their own distinct symbol or subcategory, rather than being combined with verb form or verb tense. For example, conditional, modal, passive, and subject–verb agreement are in categories separate from verb form or verb tense. The reason for this division is that students need to study each of these types of errors separately, since each has its own distinct set of rules and each creates different kinds of problems for ESL students.

ESL Grading Symbols

GLOBAL ERRORS—more serious errors
(These errors usually impede understanding.)

SYMBOL	EXPLANATION	PAGE*
vt	incorrect verb tense	1
vf	verb incorrectly formed	27
modal	incorrect use or formation of a modal	45
cond	incorrect use or formation of a conditional sentence	67
ss	incorrect sentence structure	87
wo	incorrect or awkward word order	109
conn	incorrect or missing connector	127
pass	incorrect formation or use of passive voice	147
unclear	unclear message	163

LOCAL ERRORS—less serious errors
(These errors, while distracting, most often do not impede understanding.)

SYMBOL	EXPLANATION	PAGE*
sv	incorrect subject–verb agreement	169
art	incorrect or missing article	181
num	problem with the singular or plural of a noun	197
wc	wrong word choice, including prepositions	209
wf	wrong word form	221
nonidiom	nonidiomatic (not expressed this way in English)	237

*Note: The pages listed in the right-hand column refer to pages in *Writing Clearly: An Editing Guide,* where a full explanation of each error is given.

OTHER ERRORS
(These errors are commonly made by native speakers.)

SYMBOL	EXPLANATION
cap	capitalization—capital letter needed
coh	coherence—one idea does not lead to the next
cs	comma splice—two independent clauses joined by a comma
dm	dangling modifier—phrase or clause with no word(s) to modify in a sentence
frag	fragment—incomplete sentence
lc	lower case—word(s) incorrectly capitalized
p	punctuation—punctuation incorrect or missing
pro ref pro agree	pronoun reference/agreement—pronoun reference unclear or agreement incorrect
ro	run-on—two independent clauses joined with no punctuation
sp	spelling error—word incorrectly spelled

You will see in the example sentences below how to locate and identify ESL sentence errors, using a method that is designed to be *user-friendly* for the student.

Locate the Error

In order to indicate to the student where the error is located, choose one of the following:

- **Use only the symbol to locate the error.** If the error involves one word only, you may find that simply putting the grading symbol over the error is enough indication of location.

   vt
   I am a student here at UC Davis since 1991.

- **Underline the error.**

   cond   *cond*
   If Kennedy did not visit Dallas in 1963, he might not be

   assassinated as he was at the time.

   Underlining is effective when the error involves several words together, such as several words in a verb phrase, a verb + preposition combination, or two connectors in a sentence that do not work together.

- **Bracket the part of the sentence that the error involves.**

   Unlike Hong Kong, the streets here are busy yet quiet, and
                    unclear
   [only solitude cars are on their wheels.]

   As you can see, brackets here allow you to show the student which part of the sentence is unclear. Bracketing is most helpful with errors that involve many words in a sentence or with sentence structure errors that often encompass many smaller errors in a sentence.

Identify the Error

In order to identify the error for the student, choose one of the following:

- **Write the grading symbol over the error.**

                                                   vf
   Another factor which may make an individual becoming a

   workaholic is the sense of insecurity.

- If the error involves several words, put the symbol in the middle of the set of words.

  If Kennedy <u>did not visit</u> $\overset{cond}{}$ Dallas in 1963, he <u>might not be</u> $\overset{cond}{}$

  <u>assassinated</u> as he was at the time.

- If an error involves a large number of words or actually the whole sentence, **place the symbol over the group of words where the most significant problem is located.**

  [Besides, l$\overset{ss}{}$ike Ford, the founder and head of a New York modeling

  agency, claims that nothing can interest her except working.]

- If an error involves only a part of one word (such as a missing or incorrect ending), **put the symbol over the problem area.** You can also underline the erroneous part of the word, if you wish.

  Another factor which may make an individual becom<u>ing</u> $\overset{vf}{}$ a

  workaholic is the sense of insecurity.

▼ Background/Theory: Methods of marking errors vary widely from writing in the correct form above the error to simply putting an "X" in the margin to indicate that an error of some kind has occurred somewhere in that line. However, research suggests that an optimal system of marking a paper is **indirect** rather than **direct** (Lalande 1982; Hendrickson 1980b; Walz 1982). That is, instead of directly correcting the error by rewriting, it is best to choose an indirect method, ranging from the least salient method of only indicating that an error exists to the most salient method of indicating, locating, and identifying the error. Using the indirect method, the instructor may 1) simply indicate in an end comment that a certain error is prevalent throughout the paper; 2) locate the error by circling it, underlining it, or putting an "X" in the margin; or 3) identify the located error with a grading symbol. The most frequently suggested method of these indirect methods (the method used in our system) is to indicate, locate, and identify the error (Walz 1982).

Example Sentences Showing Errors Marked

Look over the 15 example sentences below, which illustrate how you can mark sentence errors using the 15 grading symbols. (If you wish, you can remove the grading symbols and then use the example sentences below to teach students in class how to identify the 15 types of sentence errors. These examples will help students understand the grading symbols once you begin using them on their papers.)

Examples of Global Errors——(more serious—usually impede understanding)

1. **(vt) verb tense**

   I am a student here at UC Davis since 1986. *[vt over "am"]*

2. **(vf) verb form**

   Unlike me, Khan Duong did not received any training in *[vf over "received"]*

   English when she was in Vietnam.

   Another factor which may make an individual becoming a *[vf over "becoming"]*

   workaholic is the sense of insecurity.

   The other alternative is to tax more to compensate the deficit. *[vf (verb + prep) over "to compensate"]*

3. **(modal) modal**

   Chinese people think that a stranger who greets you without

   any reason must has some bad intentions. *[modal over "must has"]*

4. **(cond) conditional**

   If Kennedy did not visit Dallas in 1963, he might not be *[cond over "did not visit" and cond over "might not be"]*

   assassinated as he was at the time.

5. (ss) sentence structure

ss
[Besides, like Ford, the founder and head of a New York modeling

agency, claims that nothing can interest her except working.]

ss
[When we meet new people and start living in a totally new

environment are scary.]

ss
[The thought of my writing will put smiles on people's face

motivates me to write well.]

6. (wo) word order

wo
Students have to ask themselves [what courses are they

going to take.]

7. (conn) connector

conn
Even though she became deeply involved in her work again,
conn
but she was herself, still energetic and driven.

8. (pass) passive

pass
If a student overcomes with his financial problems, he or she

cannot concentrate on studying.

pass
A power failure was occurred last night in the dorms.

9. (unclear) unclear

Unlike Hong Kong, the streets here are busy yet quiet, and
unclear
[only solitude cars are on their wheels.]

Examples of Local Errors—(less serious—distracting yet usually do not impede understanding)

10. **(sv) subject–verb agreement**

    Yet what I saw when I came out of the airport five months ago

    sv
    were totally different from what I expected.

11. **(art) article**

    Students may like mathematics because it is $\land$ straight-

    art

    forward subject.

12. **(num) number**

    num
    With this sophisticated equipments...

    num
    The two most important reason...

13. **(wc) word choice**

    I think it is only wise to take advantage of the technology

    wc
    that is possible to us.

14. **(wf) word form**

    wf
    Because of my confident in speaking English, I have made a

    great many friends in America.

15. **(nonidiom) nonidiomatic expression**

    nonidiom
    [It takes one's courage in both hands] to leave his family and

    start life all over again in another country.

Why Use the Grading Symbols to Locate and Identify Errors?

The Discovery Process. Marking systematically with grading symbols in the way suggested above helps students make their analysis of errors a discovery process whereby they take an active role in analyzing their own problems with errors, thus making them responsible in large part for their own learning. Once you have located and identified errors for the student, he or she must then take the responsibility to learn what the symbols mean, discover exactly what his or her particular errors are, and then take the steps needed to reduce these errors.

If you wish, you can take this discovery process one step further by marking sentence-level errors in only one paragraph and then suggesting that the student use the comments on the marked paragraph as a guide to identifying possible problem areas in the rest of the paper.

Grading Symbols and Consistency. Students learn much more efficiently when you use the same set of grading symbols on all papers throughout the term. You and your colleagues may also all choose to use this same set of grading symbols for ESL papers. This type of consistency throughout a program will be helpful for students, since each term they will be working with symbols they have already seen or will see again in future classes in a writing program.

Step 3: Decide When You Will Mark Errors

Should You Mark Errors on Early Drafts?

On early drafts, the primary focus of feedback should be on content, although some instructors may choose to mark some frequent errors that impede understanding (global errors) or note in an end comment that one type of error is prevalent throughout the draft.

Should You Mark Errors on Later Drafts?

On later drafts as well as on graded papers, if there are few problems in organization and development, marking a number of sentence-level errors is entirely appropriate. However, while attending to errors in a student's paper, ensure that his or her focus on errors does not detract from the primary focus, the content of the paper.

Step 4:   Decide If Others Will Also Identify or Mark Errors

Who Should Identify or Mark Errors?

Other readers, including tutors and peers, especially after they have been trained, can also take an active part in indicating or marking errors that need attention. If your school has a tutoring program, you may want to share the error analysis system in this book with tutors in the program. After even a one-hour workshop, tutors can begin to feel comfortable in helping students work on errors using the systematic approach described in Chapter 6. Tutors might indicate to the student that certain predominant errors occur in a draft, or they might mark a few errors of a certain type in a paragraph, for example.

Students in peer response groups can also help one another locate sentence errors in drafts, but caution students against a too-early focus on sentences in peer response groups. For example, you might have students work on drafts in peer response groups in two stages. In the first stage, they could respond to content in each other's drafts. After revising their drafts for content, they could then respond to sentence problems in drafts. In this latter stage, you may choose to direct students to identify all sentence problems, to identify only global sentence errors, or to look for and identify only a select type of sentence problem, such as one recently covered in class. Students might point out for each other sentences that have problems, for example, or put a note in the margin stating that verb tense problems occur in a paragraph.

▼ **Background/Theory:** For more details about how tutors, peers, and others can become involved in the error identification process, see Hendrickson 1980a & b; and Walz 1982.

After Marking Errors

After you have marked sentence errors, you can, if you wish, assist your students in a limited way by helping them learn how they can benefit from the feedback you have given them by using the Error Awareness Sheet (which is fully illustrated in Chapter 5 and explained in Chapter 6 of this text and also in

Writing Clearly: An Editing Guide) and/or by giving them further feedback about their errors in the end comment of the paper. If you wish to help the student move beyond seeing his or her errors identified and into the discovery process of error analysis, this process is fully explained in Chapter 6. In Chapter 4, the next chapter, you will learn how to use an end comment to respond to content and to sentences as well as to explain the assigned grade.

■ CHAPTER 4: Combining Response to Content and Response to Sentences in an End Comment

In Chapter 2 of this text, you read about responding to content and, in Chapter 3, you read about responding to sentence-level features of ESL papers. This chapter explains how to combine response to content and to sentences in an end comment, a final comment on a student's paper that summarizes the strengths and weaknesses of the paper.

Along with responding to content and to sentence-level features, instructors may also need to assign grades to ESL papers. This chapter will, first, cover how to determine grades on ESL papers, in particular how to determine the effect of ESL sentence-level errors on the grade of a paper. Then, it will cover how to write full end comments which incorporate the grade (if needed), along with response to content and sentence-level features. If you are not required to assign grades to ESL papers, you will still find useful suggestions in this chapter on putting your overall response to a paper in an end comment.

This chapter is divided into two parts. If you are not required to assign grades to ESL papers, skip Part 1 and move immediately on to Part 2 on writing complete end comments.

Part 1: *Determining the Effect of ESL Sentence-Level Errors on the Grade of a Paper*

Part 2: *Writing End Comments That Incorporate Response to Content, Response to Sentence-Level Features, and the Grade*

Part 1: Determining the Effect of ESL Sentence-Level Errors on the Grade of a Paper

The task of assigning grades to papers is often the most challenging aspect of responding to ESL papers. ESL papers often do not fit neatly into any one grade category. Instead, ESL papers can often be strong in terms of content yet weak in terms of sentence-level features, leaving the instructor to decide how to weigh the strengths and weaknesses of these two aspects of the paper in determining the grade. While content is of primary importance in judging a paper, ESL sentence errors should still be taken into consideration since these errors, even when they are local (less serious), can be highly distracting to the reader. More importantly, when they are global (more serious), these errors can impede the reader's understanding of the writer's ideas.

However, many instructors, experienced ESL instructors included, find it difficult to determine just how much effect ESL errors should have on the grade of a paper, especially when there is great disparity between what the student is able to do with content versus how much control the student has in terms of language. To help you decide just how much to weigh ESL sentence errors in determining the grade of a paper, consider the following questions:

A. Are the sentence errors global or local?

B. Do the sentence errors dominate the paper?

C. Would a split grade be best for a paper?

A. Are the sentence errors global or local?

In determining the effect of errors on the grade of an ESL paper, you should distinguish between global and local errors. Frequent global errors in a paper significantly affect its readability, even when the organization and development are strong. As a result, frequent global errors usually significantly affect the grade, depending on the level of the composition class (whether it is beginning, intermediate, or advanced ESL or a freshman or upper division college composition class) and on the grading standards of the program.

Local errors usually affect a paper's grade to a lesser extent, although frequent local errors may have a more significant effect on the grade. Infrequent local errors, on the other hand, may not affect the grade at all in a strong paper.

In sum, global errors, even when infrequent, usually have an effect on the grade of a paper, while local errors most likely have an effect on the grade only if they are frequent. Yet, as mentioned above, the exact effect of both global and local errors on the grade will vary depending upon whether the student is, for example, at the beginning levels of an ESL language program or at the higher levels of a native-speaker composition program. Clearly, the needs of students in these different types of writing classes may differ and the standards for grading may differ as well, and these differences must be considered in assigning grades. An instructor teaching a group of students studying English only for the summer in an intensive English program, for example, may choose not to grade these students as strictly as a class of students preparing to do graduate work at an American university or preparing to take the TOEFL Test of Written English.

B. Do sentence-level errors dominate the paper?

Deciding whether or not sentence-level errors dominate the paper overall also helps in determining how much effect the sentence-level errors have on the grade. You will most likely find it easy to assign a high grade to a paper with strong organization and development and few serious ESL errors, or a low grade to a paper in which serious ESL errors make the paper largely incomprehensible. However, perhaps the most problematic paper to grade is the one with frequent ESL errors but strong organization and development. With this type of paper, you will want to consider the dominant impression of the paper—that is, whether the sentence errors dominate the paper overall.

In a paper in which the errors dominate, the errors will be so distracting that you will be highly aware of them while reading. This sense of frequent distraction will build until the overall effect at the end of the paper is that the paper is dominated by ESL errors. However strong the content may be, your attention is continuously drawn to sentence errors rather than to the ideas the writer is expressing. The difficulty in determining a grade on this type of paper is that the paper is unbalanced; it has strong content but weak sentences. With this kind of paper, the grade may more closely reflect the domination of error rather than the strengths in content. In other words, the grade may not be an exact average of strong content and weak sentences.

C. Would a split grade be best for a paper?

Some instructors resolve the dilemma of weighing both content and sentences by assigning two grades to a paper, one for content and one for sentences. The benefit of this method is that the student is rewarded for what he or she has done well. The drawback of assigning two grades is that the student may get the impression that content and sentences are distinct rather than interwoven entities which function together to make up a piece of writing. Also, the student receiving a split grade may rejoice in the "A" and ignore the "D," thus not seeing the necessity of working on the weaknesses in his or her writing. Therefore, many program administrators advise that instructors decide on a single grade, rather than give a split grade on a paper.

▼ **Note:** Many composition instructors find it particularly useful to use a set of written grading standards to help them grade ESL papers. Grading standards provide instructors with criteria they can use to assign grades to ESL papers as consistently as possible within a class or across several classes in a program. If you are interested in developing grading standards either for yourself or for your program, please see the Appendix in this text. It covers what grading standards are, gives guidelines for developing them, and contains three sets of sample grading standards that have been developed for use in actual writing programs.

Part 2: Writing End Comments That Incorporate Response to Content, Response to Sentence-Level Features, and the Grade

In addition to responding to content and sentence-level features in the margins or within the text of a paper, you will usually want to summarize your overall response to content and language in an end comment. In the end comment, you can summarize the strengths and weaknesses of a paper in terms of both content and sentence-level features. You can also, if appropriate, suggest strategies for revision to the student.

If you are responding to the final draft of a paper (the draft students are submitting for a grade), then you will probably want to incorporate all of the following into the end comment:

A. Response to content

B. Response to sentence-level features

C. The grade, as well as some justification of the grade

If you are not assigning a grade to a paper or are responding to an ungraded draft of a paper, you will still often want to write an end comment. In this case, the suggestions in Parts A and B of this section are useful.

A. Including response to content in the end comment

In the end comment, you should respond first to the content of a paper because, as noted earlier, content is ultimately the most important part of the paper. In responding to content, keep in mind the benefits discussed in previous chapters of establishing a positive affective climate by first responding positively as an interested reader. Once this positive affective climate is established, then point out weaknesses in content, including organization and development.

B. Including response to sentences in the end comment

Next, you will want to respond to the sentence-level features of a paper. Keep the following guidelines in mind:

1. Balance positive and negative feedback on sentences.

2. Indicate, if appropriate, the effect of sentence-level errors on the grade.

1. Balance positive and negative feedback on sentences.

Whenever possible, give both positive and negative feedback on sentences. You might, for example, begin or end the sentence-level comments with positive feedback, such as "You have made great progress in controlling your verb tenses in this paper."

In giving negative feedback on sentences, your aim is usually to draw the student's attention to his or her most serious and frequent errors. Even if you have marked sentence-level errors on the paper itself, in most cases you will still want to draw the student's attention to the most serious and frequent errors in the end comment. This helps the student know which errors he or she should begin working on first. When pointing out a student's most serious and frequent errors, limit the focus to just a few errors, since realistically most ESL students can work on only a few errors at a time.

2. Indicate the effect of sentence-level errors on the grade.

If sentence-level errors significantly weaken a paper and thus affect the grade, you should make this fact clear to the student. Likewise, if a student has significantly improved his or her sentence-level work, either from earlier drafts or from previous papers, point out this improvement, noting its general effect on the grade, if appropriate.

C. Including the grade, and perhaps some justification of the grade, in the end comment

To help a student see exactly what he or she needs to work on and also to prevent disputes over grades, you may feel the need to justify the grade you have assigned to a paper in the end comment. You may, for example, want to emphasize that weaknesses in content have caused a particular paper to fall below the passing mark or that sentence-level errors have caused the grade to drop significantly. In these cases, it is always best to be as specific and forth-right as possible in identifying those weaknesses that have had the most significant effect on the grade.

It is equally important to point out exactly what has made a paper receive a high grade. In this case, a clear focus on the student's strengths enables the student to build on these strengths. For instance, if a student becomes conscious of his or her ability to use effective specific details, he or she will be motivated to continue using them in future writing.

If you are using written grading standards (as mentioned in Part 1 of this chapter and explained fully in the Appendix of this book), you may wish to further justify the grade on a paper by quoting appropriate phrases or sentences from the grading standards.

In the two sample end comments that follow, you will see how an instructor has incorporated response to both content and sentence-level features on two different papers—one a very effective paper and the other a weaker paper. Note that, in each of these end comments, the instructor refers to the grade on the paper, making it clear to the student why the paper has been assigned either a high or a low grade.

Sample End Comment 1

In the following end comment, the instructor incorporates response to both content and sentence-level features. The instructor also justifies a high grade to the student.

> *Your analysis of how your father and mother helped you develop a love of learning was very nicely done. The specifics you used about how your father's guitar playing made you want to learn to play the guitar put the reader right in the living room with your mother and you.*
>
> *The earlier draft of this paper had problems in verb tense shifting that made it hard for the reader to know whether you were talking about the past or present. In this final draft, verb tenses are used*

effectively. The scattered errors in number and word form are few and usually do not distract the reader. Keep up the good work in editing your papers for verb tense and verb form errors!

As you can see from the high grade on this paper, your careful job of revising both for content and language resulted in a very effective paper. I enjoyed reading it.

Sample End Comment 2

In the following end comment, the instructor incorporates response to content and sentence-level features. The instructor also justifies a low grade to the student.

In this essay you make several very strong points about the topic of suicide—about the pain of family and friends left behind and about the help that is available.

Several weaknesses in development and sentences, however, keep the essay below the passing mark. You do stay focused on the thesis of your essay, yet evidence and analysis are lacking on several points. Also, frequent global sentence-level errors (especially verb tense, sentence structure, and unclear sentences) often make it difficult for the reader to understand your good ideas.

In Chapter 5 of this book, you will find a variety of sample student papers from different types of programs and from different levels. The end comments on these papers will serve as further examples of how various instructors try to make all the components of the end comment work together. While these papers have not been given grades, they illustrate how to incorporate response to content and response to sentence-level features in end comments.

In Chapter 6 of this book, which covers ways you can help your students work on their sentence-level errors, you will find suggestions for incorporating strategies the student can use for effectively working on his or her sentence-level errors into your end comments.

■ CHAPTER 5:   Sample Papers

In the previous chapters, you have seen sample papers and end comments illustrating the response system in this text. In Chapter 2 you read two sample papers with responses to content only, and in Chapter 4 you read two sample papers and comments that responded to content and to language. The end comments for each paper incorporated a justification for the grade, response to content, and response to sentence-level features. In this chapter, you will find eight sample papers that illustrate how instructors can respond to student writing using the system in this text.

These sample papers represent a variety of programs and levels. The first three papers come from a three-course series of ESL composition classes at the university level (beginning, intermediate, and advanced levels). Papers Four and Five come from a basic writing class and a freshman composition class at the university level. The sixth paper comes from a multi-skills ESL course for international graduate students who are currently enrolled at the university level. The seventh paper comes from an intensive English program and the eighth paper from an ESL composition course at a junior college. You will note that grades have not been included in the end comments of these papers because grades vary widely from level to level and from program to program.

Reading these sample papers and using them as a reference tool will help you familiarize yourself with putting the grading symbols into practice and writing end comments that respond to content and sentence-level features, justify a grade, and involve the student in the process of error analysis.

In the following parts, you will learn how reading the sample papers will help you.

Part 1: *How the Sample Papers Will Help You Work with the Grading Symbols*

Part 2: *How the Sample Papers Will Help You Write an End Comment That Incorporates Content, Sentence-Level Features, and Justification of a Grade*

Part 3: *How the Sample Papers Will Show You Ways to Write an End Comment That Will Help the Student Begin the Process of Error Analysis*

Part I: How the Sample Papers Will Help You Work With the Grading Symbols

By seeing how other instructors have used the grading symbols in these sample papers, you will become familiar with using the symbols consistently and accurately. You will also increase your ability to recognize the errors that correspond to the symbols for the 15 errors that you studied in Chapter 3.

By observing how other instructors have chosen to mark errors in these eight papers, you will learn to decide how many errors to mark in an ESL paper (how to mark selectively) and how to make the following decisions relative to marking errors:

- when and how to mark selectively for global errors only

- when to mark both global and local errors selectively

- when to mark most errors

Part 2: How the Sample Papers Will Help You Write an End Comment That Incorporates Content, Sentence-Level Features, and Justification of a Grade

Reading this selection of eight end comments will give you a broader idea of what you learned in Chapter 4 about writing an end comment that incorporates response to content and error as well as justification of a grade (if desired or necessary). You will see the following illustrated:

- how to respond to the content of a paper, addressing both its strengths and weaknesses

- how to respond to sentence-level features in a paper (both sentence-level strengths and sentence-level errors)

- how to tie together response to content and to error

- how to indicate to the student the ways in which the strengths and/or weaknesses of the paper have affected the grade

Part 3: How the Sample Papers Will Show You Ways to Write an End Comment That Will Help the Student Begin the Process of Error Analysis

Seeing what other instructors have written in the end comments of these sample papers can serve as a guide to show you how to indicate to the student ways for him or her to begin to take responsibility for error analysis. You will see illustrations of the following:

- how to help the student decide which errors to work on first

- how to indicate to the student where to get help on sentence-level errors (for example, to direct the student to a tutor, a specific unit in *Writing Clearly: An Editing Guide,* or to invite the student to come to office hours)

You will also see an example of an Error Awareness Sheet that has been filled in for Paper Five.

Sample Paper One

Class:

This out-of-class paper was written by a student in the beginning level of a three-course series of ESL composition classes at the university level. These undergraduate composition classes are part of a composition program in a university English department.

Notes on Instructor's Response:

This paper has been marked selectively for global errors, although a few local errors have been marked. Also, in the end comments, the instructor has indicated which errors this beginning-level student needs to work on first.

Writing Topic:

Write a paragraph in which you analyze a character trait that you admire in yourself or a friend.

MY FRIEND FONG

One of the character trait I admire most about my friend Fong is his
                        ss   vt
sense of humor. [Fong and I, we] grow up in the same neighborhood,

and we are very good friend. Fong is funny and always finds a joke to

say, no matter what my mood is. He always finds something to make
                        vf (verb + prep)
me laugh, though I try not. Last year, on a sunny week-end [Fong and
ss
I, we] went fishing. But the night just before, my girlfriend called me

and said that we should not see each other anymore. She did not give
                                                              vt
any explanation and while I was asking some questions, she hang up.
                conn
The next morning, as Fong came to pick me up for fishing, he noticed
            nonidiomatic   vf
that [I had a bad mood.] He asked what had happen to me, and I just

said, "Nothing." "If nothing had happened to you," he said, "your nose

would not be that red and your ears that big." Though I tried hard not
vf (verb + no prep)   *ss (...so...that)*
to laugh, I couldn't <u>resist to</u> his joke. *[*Fong also kept me busy with all

kind of jokes the entire day that I forgot about my sad mood.*]* We

fished and laughed the whole day, but did not catch any fish. When we
wc
came back home, I was already reconforted for what my girl had told

me on the previous night. I did not know how to thank Fong and his
wf   *vf*
joke. But Fong and his humoristic charater will always be engrave in

my heart because when we are together and when I am having a hard

time or pressure, he will always find a way to relieve me and make me

laugh.

Great
example!

End Comment:

Overall, this is a very clear paragraph with a wonderfully vivid example about Fong's sense of humor. (This must make him indeed a treasured friend.) I also like your analysis, especially the idea that his humorous character will always be engraved in your heart.

Sentence-level problems do, however, seriously weaken the paragraph. You will want to work especially hard on sentence structure, verb form, and verb tense problems.

Sample Paper Two

Class:

This out-of-class paper was written by a student in the intermediate level of a three-course series of ESL composition classes at the university level. These undergraduate composition classes are part of a composition program in a university English department.

Notes on Instructor's Response:

This paper has been marked selectively for global errors, although some local errors have been marked. The following native-speaker errors have also been marked: *CS* (comma splice, two independent clauses joined with a comma); *coherence* (one idea does not lead to the next idea); *fragment* (an incomplete sentence); and *SV* (subject and verb do not agree). In the end comment, the instructor first responds positively as an interested reader and then notes the paper's weaknesses in focus. On sentences, the instructor points out an area of improvement and then indicates the sentences errors that need work first.

Writing Topic:

First, think of an important decision that you or your family has made. Next, write an essay analyzing two or three reasons for this decision.

Two Reasons Students Choose UC Davis

"Look! Did you have a problem choosing the college? [After you
frag
graduated from high school?"] I did. I remember when I was in high

school, I always worried about what college I wanted to apply to after

my high school graduation. I began to apply to UC Davis and UC Santa
vf (verb + prep)
Cruz during my senior year. But I got accepted both UCD and UCSC. I
ss
decided to go to UC Davis because [UC Davis it closer] to my family. I
coherence
could go back and forth everyday if I wanted. The two reasons that

num

many student choose UC Davis are the peaceful quiet college town and

the excellent faculty.

One of the reasons that many student choose UCD *[*are the peaceful *ss*

quiet college town.*]* For example, I like UCD because UCD is located

in the quiet college town. There is a lot of farm land around UCD. Also
                                                              cs
there is no traffic around at UCD town, when I have time, I can ride my

bike around UCD town. Sometimes I ride my bike around the farm and
              vf   *vf*
see the cows. I <u>was enjoy</u> <u>to see</u> all kind of animal a lot. Also many

student choose UCD because it's easy to concentrate on homework. On
                                              wf
the other hand, at UC Santa Cruz it is very noise. Beside all the noise,

there is a nice beach around. It is very difficult to concentrate because of
         vf   *cond*
that noise came from the beach. If I had time I rather go to the beach

and get some fresh air rather than review for my midterm next week.
                                                        coherence
However, in UC Davis there is no other activity beside studying. I

realize many students choose UCD because it is a quiet place.

The most important reason why many student choose UCD is the

excellent faculty. For example, I remember last quarter I was having a

trouble picking my classes. I didn't know what to do because I didn't
                                              unclear
know anybody around UCD that much. *[*I didn't who would ask the
                                              unclear
question about my classes.*]* Beside my faculty advisor, *[*I didn't anyone

as much as.*]* I made an appointment to see my faculty adviser.
   conn   *vt*
Conversely, I am a kind of afraid because I didn't know what my faculty
   vt   *modal*   *vf/vt*
adviser look like. I was afraid she yelled at me because I picking a

vt
wrong classes for my major requirements. When I see my faculty adviser
vt   *vt*   *vf*
face to face, he is very nice and help me picking all the right classes I

wanted to take for my major. Also he showed me how to take the classes
               ss
to prepare for my General Education classes. Also [he told me don't

take] the General Education classes until I passed my English A class.
unclear   *coherence*   *num*
[I didn't until my faculty adviser told me.] I realize many student is

very happy about their own faculty adviser.
              sv
   In conclusion I realize many students is very happy about choosing

UC Davis because it has a quiet college town. Many student can con-
                        wf
centrate on homework easily because there is no noisy and no other
       ss
activity. Also [many student happy at UCD] because it has excellent

faculty.

End Comment:

I really enjoyed reading your paper about why students choose UC Davis. Thesis and topic sentences are very clear, and you do a good job of using specific details. I enjoyed the example about your riding your bike around the farms and seeing cows, as well as the very vivid example about your faculty advisor. However, this paper drifts away from its overall focus (why students choose UC Davis) and instead focuses on why you like UC Davis now. In addition, in the paragraph about excellent faculty, the focus becomes too narrow, concentrating only on faculty advising.

You've really improved control of verb tense since your last paper. Now you'll want to concentrate on mastering problems with sentence structure and verb form. These problems distract the reader from your lively writing style and your good ideas. Eventually, you'll also want to work on coherence problems, which you'll see identified in the opening and body paragraphs. Come to see me if you would like to discuss any of these problems.

Sample Paper Three

Class:

This out-of-class paper was written by a student in the advanced level of a three-course series of ESL composition classes at the university level. These undergraduate ESL composition classes are part of a composition program in a university English department.

Notes on Instructor's Response:

This paper has been marked selectively for global errors. Also, in the end comment, the instructor has indicated which errors this advanced-level student should work on first.

Writing Topic:

In her essay, "Listening," Eudora Welty describes how she developed a love of reading and of learning. She credits her parents for giving her the love for books and writing she has today, a respect for the written word that developed because her parents were willing to share with her their love of reading and of learning.

Write an essay in which you discuss a person or persons in your life who have helped you develop a love of learning, analyzing how this person or persons have helped you develop a respect for reading and writing.

A LOVE OF LEARNING

In the essay "Listening," Eudora Welty recalled a memorable learn-
vf
ing experience by describing how her parents helped her developed a

love of reading and of learning by sharing their love of reading and

writing with her. Recalling a memorable learning experience is quite

easy for me because I know I will never forget Tony. Tony was my tutor

when I was in Hong Kong. She not only helped me with my English

conn (not only...but also)   vf

and Chinese, she also helped me developed a love of learning and a

respect of reading and writing through her two years of tutoring.   *Good thesis*

vf

    The love that Tony had for teaching helped me developed the love of

learning. Tony started tutoring me when I was in fourth grade. She

came to teach me and help me twice a week. Each lesson was about two

vf

hours. Within this two hours, she would help me solved the problems

that I had in my schoolwork by explaining the problems thoroughly. If

ss

I didn't understand the problem [by the first time she explained,] she

would explain it again and again until I totally understood it. Some-

vt   vf   pass

times she help me prepared the next coming chapter [that it was going

to cover] in school. Every week she would bring me to the public

library at least for an hour. She would assign a few books for me to read

vf

in order to help me developed a reading habit. The patience and the

vt   cond

smile that Tony always had had encouraged me to learn. I wouldn't

afraid to ask her questions if I didn't understand because I knew she

would try to help me as much as she could. To me, Tony wasn't only a

tutor; she was a good teacher and a nice friend. The way she taught, the

vt   vf

patience she had and her love of teaching had helped me developed the

love of learning.

vt + not pass

    At the same period of time, my interest on reading had been devel-

oped also because of Tony. Every week Tony would bring me to a

public library at least for a hour. She would tell me to pick a book that

I wanted to read in Chinese first and then she would tell me to read it in

English after I knew the story. It was interesting that I preferred the

vt

story format in English rather than in Chinese. I thought it was because

the English one was the original one and it had more details and de-

scriptions in the story. By that time, I loved to read fairy-tale. I loved

all the fantastic stories and the characters in them. Sometimes I would

daydream that I was the character in the book, especially those beauti-

ful princess. I liked to put myself into the story, and I found that I <u>was</u>

vf

<u>so enjoyed</u> while I was reading. Starting at that particular time, I began

to like reading because of the enjoyment I had from it.

vf

Tony not only helped me developed my reading habit, but she also

vf

helped me developed my writing skills both in English and Chinese.

She did not look at my problem as a writing or composition weakness,

but rather as a thinking problem. She taught me how to think care-

fully, logically and sensibly. She started giving me a few details of an

vf

event and asked me arrange them in an essay format, according to their

importance. As I was beginning to understand the procedure, she would

just give me a topic and instruct me to brainstorm it first, then arrange

my own ideas in order. Through these practices, my writing skills

conn

improved. <u>Not only that,</u> the time it took for me to start an essay <u>had</u>

vt

<u>decreased</u> dramatically. Because of the improvement that I had in my

vt + not passive

writing skills, my interest on writing <u>had been developed</u>.

Tony, who spent a vast amount of time teaching me and helping me

develop a love of learning and a love of reading and writing, was very

Aren't you thinking about this <u>now</u>?

conn

special. I respected her as my teacher and my sister also. <u>Since</u> we are in

conn

two different places right now, <u>so</u> the respect I have on her have been

ss

transferred on reading and writing. I'm so glad [that I had Tony been

my totur] for two years. I learned a lot from her and I know I will never

forget her.

End Comment:

Your focus on Tony's role in helping you develop a love of learning is very nicely done. It seems that Tony did a good job of teaching you thinking skills. Also, your comparison of reading the same story in Chinese and English is very interesting. There is, however, some over-lap between the points in body paragraphs one and two about going to the library. As part of strengthening your vocabulary skills, you will want to make it a practice to find synonyms for words you use often in an essay instead of repeating the same word; in rereading your paper, think about different words you could use instead of repeating the word "help."

The numerous sentence-level errors significantly weaken this paper, drawing the reader's attention away from your interesting ideas. I have only marked the most serious global errors in this paper, and I suggest that out of these you begin working with your tutor on verb form and verb tense and then later on sentence structure, passive, and connectors.

Note: After "help," you need the base form of the verb (She helped me develop). See verb form in Writing Clearly: An Editing Guide.

Sample Paper Four

Class:

This in-class essay was written by a student in a basic writing class at the university level.

Notes on the Instructor's Response:

In addition to pointing out the strengths and weaknesses in content, the instructor very clearly indicates that the numerous serious sentence-level errors keep the essay from passing. The instructor has also chosen to mark mostly global errors.

In responding to sentence-level errors, the instructor has marked two native-speaker errors. *P* indicates that a punctuation mark, in this case a comma, is missing. *CS* means comma splice, a sentence boundary problem in which two independent clauses have been incorrectly joined with a comma.

Writing Topic:

Write an essay in which you analyze the effects reading had on Richard Wright's life.

(In the essay, "The Library Card," Richard Wright describes how he began to read a great deal and how this reading affected his views of the world around him and the place of the black man in that world.)

THE EFFECTS OF READING

vt
In Richard Wright's essay "The Library Card", Wright talked about

his feelings after reading. He got the positive result [of able to learn
ss
about other people and see life's possibilities for himself.] But on the
modal (vf)
other hand, since he lived in the south, he had to disguised himself [to
ss
be unbookish.]
conn   *vt*
∧Reading had enabled Wright to learn about people. Reading about
vf
different characters could make one to understand different personality.

When one encountered a similar character in real life, he could [refer

vt ⸻ *modal*

unclear ⸻ *vt*

back to the personality,] and therefore had a better understanding of

people. After reading Sinclair Lewis's Main Street, Richard identified

his white boss as an American type. Richard felt that he knew him and

unclear

the limits of his life. [This was all contributed to a similar character

p

George F. Babbit that Richard read.] Before Richard had felt the "vast

distance" seperating him from the boss. Now he could look at the boss

feeling closer to him because he knew exactly [what type of character

ss

was him.] This was one of the result from Richard's reading.

> *Good example about Wright's boss, but explain "the limits."*

> *Good analysis*

Besides learning about other people, Richard also learned the possi-

bilities of life for him from reading. Reading opened up Richard's view

vf (verb + prep)

for life, and made him think what he wanted to do with his life. For

example, Richard realized that he had choices of staying the way he

ss

was, fighting the whites or leaving the south. [Before started reading,]

cs

he only knew one way to survive, that was being a black in south. Now,

modal (vf)

he understood that he could chose according to what he wanted from

life. That was a big step for him. Finally, he chose to leave the south for

his own sake.

> *Good specifics and analysis*

p

Regardless the good results reading also brought negative results for

unclear

Richard, [like disguised himself to be unbookish.] Since blacks were

vf ⸻ *pass*

"suppose" to be uneducated, whites were expected blacks to be mind-

less or they would be punished. Even though Richard gained all the

knowledge from reading, he could not show it. When Mr. Olin said,

> *Who is Mr. Olin?*

"You act like you've stolen something", Richard laughed because he

                                       conn

knew that was the way the white man expected him to act. For he now

had to pretend to be a black boy who wasn't educated, and didn't know

              cs   *wf*

how to think, it was hard and tired. Richard had to be "conscious" of

himself, "watch his every act" and "hide" his new knowledge every

second.

Point becomes clearer here

Very effective use of details from the reading

    From reading, Richard got positive results like <u>having</u> more knowl-

                        ss (parallel struct)

edge of people around him, and <u>realized</u> the possibilities around him.

                        vf   *vf*

He also got negative results like have to diguised himself to be

          vt   *modal*

"unbookish." I hoped he <u>could have</u> a better life in north, [where he

unclear

wasn't denied.]

Nice personal response

End Comment:

    In this essay, you analyze the Wright reading passage effectively.
Your paragraph topics are strong, with much good evidence and analy-
sis for each point. I especially like your use of specific details from the
reading passage, such as the example about Wright's boss and the de-
tails you include about Wright's having to disguise himself. However,
the point about Wright's having to disguise himself is not quite clear
initially, although it becomes somewhat clearer later.

    What keeps the essay from passing, however, is the large number of
sentence-level errors. These errors slow the reader down considerably
and often keep the reader from clearly understanding your very good
points. I've chosen to mark only the most serious and frequent errors in
this essay, including verb tense, sentence structure, and verb form. You
will want to work on these sentence-level errors first. Let's get together
in conference to discuss strategies for working on these errors.

Sample Paper Five

Class:

This out-of-class paper was written in a freshman composition class at the university level.

Notes on the Instructor's Response:

The instructor has marked most of the global and local errors in this paper, since the student has a good grasp of organization and development and the number of errors is not overwhelming. The instructor has also marked the following native speaker errors: predication (the subject and verb do not work together logically) and sp (spelling). The instructor has also chosen to fill out and attach an Error Awareness Sheet to help the student prioritize her errors.

Writing Topic:

The students were asked to write a compare/contrast paper on a topic of their own choice.

═══════════════════════

WHICH IS FOR ME?

"So have you decided which major it'll be?" My relatives, including my mother, never seem to be able to avoid this question every fall season that someone in our family is entering a college. The discussion *vt* about how to choose a major <u>would dominate</u> other topics for three months until the college application process ended in November. Until *vt* *ss* my turn to choose a major, I <u>have heard</u> their similar suggestions [many times] that I felt the process would be easy enough for me. First determine what things I enjoyed doing. Then just pick a major that closely tied with that particular interest. As it turned out, my sister made her

Nice opening!

choice easily by using a common method, while I had to <u>give</u> more

num ————————————— ss ———————————

thoughts and <u>approached</u> the problem with another process.

After all the advice from adults, my sister chose her major by using

the most straight-forward method, considering her interests. Hoping

not to have to change her major later, my sister seriously listed all her

interests from simple hobbies, such as reading, playing *art* ∧piano, to trav-

elling and business. Because my sister did her work well only if some-

thing could arouse her interests, she paid close attention to the items *num*

that she enjoyed doing the most and narrowed them down to fewer

items. From this list, she selected a career corresponding to each inter-

est and *[*discussed with my mother.*]* Finally, she decided on a business *ss*

major, accounting; her actual goal was to become a certified public

accountant (CPA). Initially, she wanted a career in traveling because it

could be fun and adventurous, but to be constantly moving from places

would never give her a real home <u>to settle</u>. Moreover, part of ∧*[*CPA *vf (verb + prep)* *art*

job description sometimes would require*]* travelling to different com- *predication*

panies in different counties or states during the auditing season any-

how. ∧She still would have her chance to travel. This process really *conn*

helped her because four years later, my sister still kept her major and

graduated with her accounting degree.

Instead of using my sister's way, I had to develop my new way. I had

my interests, then, but I was not sure if I would still be stimulated with *wc*

the same thing in the future. Since I could not decide definitely, my

relatives advised that I go in undeclared which would enable me to

Interesting example about your sister

explore other alternatives and opportunities. However, I did not want
      art   *num*
to enter a college without any directions. Then, one day, the idea struck

me: why not declare one of the most difficult majors to get in, so that
                              art
changing my major to ∧ less difficult one in the future would be easier

than trying to get into some hard major from the undeclared major. By
                                     wc
choosing my major this way, if I were to decide on other less difficult

major later, I would not have to worry about my grades as much;
  sp
oterwise if I happened to like this difficult major that I had picked, I
  modal   *wc*
could be relieved that I already got it. With that idea, I made a list of

popular, impacted majors to enable me to examine each major closely.

Then, looking at the General Catalog, I chose a major that covered a

wide range of subjects. As a result, I picked engineering because, in-
             vf (verb + no prep)
stead of [stressing on] math or science, it emphasized both math and

science classes which were necessary backgrounds for many other ma-
          nonidiomatic
jors. Now that [I am in] an engineering major, I do not worry about
                 num
trying to get into other field, because other majors are more lenient in

accepting students. If, someday, I conclude that I want to be an engi-
      vt
neer, I am happy to know that I have made it.

    Obviously, my process is time-consuming and requires constant

searching and exploring until I find what I want. I know that I will
                                    vt
eventually find my answer. Although my sister and I arrive at some
                         vt
decision about our majors, we each use our own methods that best

suited our needs. Last fall, when I heard my relatives discussing the

same, annual topic about my cousin, who was applying for college, I

A fun.
original
example

Good use of
conditional

was glad that they had their true concerns for all of us, but I was also

aware that my cousin would somehow, in her own way, find her major.

art

There will never be the best way to choose a major except that which

art

satisfies ∧ individual's personalities and needs.

> Good return
> to opening

End Comment:

I really enjoyed reading this essay and hearing about you and your sister. You include lots of interesting details about your sister's choice and then a lively and original example of your own method—fun to read!

Organization is very strong here. Also, you make a very good connection between this opening and conclusion—a vivid example.

As you can see from the attached Error Awareness Sheet, you'll want to begin working immediately on verb tense and sentence structure. As time permits, articles will also need attention. Let's get together to discuss the best strategies for attacking these problems.

This is a strong essay in terms of organization and development; however, sentence-level problems bring the grade down.

Error Awareness Sheet

Directions: This Error Awareness Sheet will help you to discover what your sentence-level errors are and to learn to prioritize them. Put a check in the second column for each error marked on your returned paper. Then, from the most frequent errors in the second column, select two or three that you can begin working on first and put a check next to them in the third column. Always remember that you need to work on frequent global errors first.

Name of Student: ░░░░░░░░░░ **Essay:** "Which Is for Me?"

TYPE OF ERROR	TOTAL NUMBER OF ERRORS	TOP-PRIORITY ERRORS TO WORK ON
GLOBAL ERRORS (more serious)		
vt	✓✓✓✓✓	✓
vf	✓✓	
modal	✓	
cond		
ss	✓✓	✓
wo		
conn		
pass		
unclear		
LOCAL ERRORS (less serious)		
sv		
art	✓✓✓✓✓✓	✓
num	✓✓✓✓	
wc	✓✓✓	
wf		
nonidiom		
OTHER ERRORS		
cap		
coh		
cs		
dm		
frag		
lc		
p		
pro ref/agree		
ro		
sp		

Sample Paper Six

Class:

This in-class response was written by an international graduate student enrolled at a university and taking a multi-skills ESL class.

Notes on the Instructor's Response:

As you will see in the end comment, the instructor has chosen to mark most of this student's sentence-level errors because of the strong organization of the essay and the student's desire to have all of his sentence-level errors marked.

In addition to marking ESL sentence-level errors, the instructor has marked several pronoun reference problems, indicating them with the symbol *pro ref*. A pronoun reference problem occurs when the noun to which a pronoun refers is not clear to the reader.

Writing Topic:

Discuss the progress you have made so far on your English 25 term paper assignment. In addition to explaining what you have already done and what you are currently working on, comment on the aspect of writing a term paper that has been most challenging for you.

MY TERM PAPER PROGRESS

         vt

After five weeks of studies at this university, I learned many skills

 art   *art*

from ∧English 25 course. One of the most important is writing∧ term

paper. I would like to write something about my term paper right now.

    vt   *wc*

I scheduled my term paper writing progress into 10 parts: 1) decid-

               num

ing topics, 2) collecting reference papers/books, 3) briefly reading those

                vf (verb + no prep)

papers/books 4) <u>writing down</u> the outline, 5) reading the papers/books

                           vf   *art*

carefully and taking notes, 6) write∧ first draft, 7) revising the draft,

8) asking my tutor to comment on my paper, 9) typing it, and

                                            vt
10) finally checking the paper. So far, I finished the first four steps and
sv   *pro ref*
is proceeding to the 5th step. I hope I can speed up; otherwise <u>it</u> will be
                wc   *ss*
very busy <u>on</u> the end of November because [it dues] on December 4.

In order to type my term paper, I must learn how to operate Macin-
                                vt
tosh or PS/2 computers because I never use them before, especially two

kinds of packages (Word 5.0 for Macintosh and Wordperfect for PS/2).
                vt?   *art*   *pro ref*
As a result, I attended several lab classes offered by ˄ computer center. <u>It</u>
                        pro ref   *pro ref*
is really interesting and I enjoyed <u>it</u> very much. <u>It</u> is useful for my
                        pro ref
future career too, and I think <u>it</u> is most challenging to me in writing

my term paper.

End Comment:

*In this response, you have done a careful job of addressing both parts
of the question and have illustrated your points with good specifics,
including the names of word-processing programs. Good organization,
too!*

*Because your organization is strong, I have marked most of your
sentence-level errors as you requested. I would suggest, however, that
you first work on verb tense, verb form, and articles. Also, you will want
to work on avoiding unclear references when you use the pronoun "it."*

Sample Paper Seven

Class:

This in-class paper was written by a student in a composition class at the advanced level in an intensive English program.

Notes on the Instructor's Response:

The instructor has chosen to mark all the global errors in this native Spanish speaker's paper. The instructor has also selectively marked one local error because this error, subject-verb agreement, can be a common error among Spanish speakers.

In addition to ESL sentence-level errors, the instructor has marked three other errors. *Pro ref* means pronoun reference and indicates that the noun to which a pronoun refers is not clear to the reader. *Frag* means fragment and indicates an incomplete sentence. *CS* means comma splice and indicates that two independent clauses have been incorrectly joined with a comma.

Writing Topic:

In the movie, *Stand and Deliver,* Mr. Escalante said to the students just before they took the Advanced Placement Exam for the second time: "You are the true dreamers. And dreams accomplish great things."

Why do you think he said that the students were true dreamers? What does that mean? Why do you think he said this to them at that particular time?

STAND AND DELIVER

"You are the true dreamers and dreams accomplish great things."

Mr. Escalante told this to his students at Garfield High School in East

Los Angeles. I asked myself, "What did he mean with this strange

sentence?" Maybe at first time that I read it, it had no meaning but now
       vt?   *vt?*

when I read it the second time, I begin to think seriously, and I think
                                  ss

it's the best sentence that a teacher can [say his students.] Why?

sv

All along the movie we can see that this group of students have a lot

cs

of problems; they don't have enough money, some of them have parents

pro ref   *pro ref*

that both work outside the home so <u>she or he</u> has to take care of <u>her or</u>

<u>his</u> brothers and sisters etc. All these situations together produce a

situation in which the students cannot study very hard and enough

hours. [Despite the fact that Mr. Escalante wants and dreams that with

frag

his help and perseverence, they could be really good students and pass

cs

the Advance Placement test.] And they do it, they pass the Advance

cs

Placement, Mr. Escalante's dream was possible. So, that is why

ss

Mr. Escalante [say that sentence his students.]

It isn't clear which clause "even though" should be attached to

In summary, if you have dreams, never give up; [even though you

frag

fall down three, four times;] stand up and go straigh because maybe one

day your dreams will be realized.

End Comment:

Clearly, you understand the movie and what Mr. Escalante wants for his students. You also have some good ideas about the problems of these students and their parents. However, it is not exactly clear why you think Mr. Escalante told his students that they were "true dreamers."

Your fluency in English is quite impressive. You will, however, need to work on sentence boundaries and verb tenses. As you have time, you can also work on the other errors marked.

Sample Paper Eight

Class:

This in-class paper was written by a student in an ESL composition course at a junior college.

Notes on Instructor's Response:

The instructor in this case has chosen to address the major weakness in this paper, the lack of focus on the question. The paper has been marked very selectively for sentence-level problems (a few global errors only) because clearly this student would be overwhelmed and unable to work on all of his errors at once.

Writing Topic:

In recent years, advances in science and technology (computers, calculators, dishwashers, washing machines, dryers, etc.) have had a tremendous impact on people's lives. Choose one technological development that has affected your life. Give reasons to explain the changes it has made in your life. How would your life be different today if you did not have the benefit of this development?

CAR

pass
There were a lot of technology which invented in the 1980's. They

were computer, T.V. and typewriter etc... Car is one of the technology.   *Are you focused on the question?*

It has affected my life because care was expensive and unsafety in my

mind.
                    unclear   *vt/vf*
    First of all, [car was expensive in mind.] I had has a 1981 Toyota   *Reader doesn't know if you still have the car because of verb tense problems.*
          vt?
cellica. I spend about two thousand for car every year. Many people
                  vf
should ask me why car was cost me so much money. I had to buy car
                                              modal
insurance and gas. Sometime the car broke down. I should buy the
          cond   *cond*   *vt*
supply to repair it. If I didn't have the car, I would have a trouble. I use

the car to drive to school, work every day. Also I lived in suburn area.
vt
That's why the car is important to me.
                                                                vt/vf
   Second of all, I think the car was unsafty. Every year car accident <u>was</u>
        vf
<u>cause</u> many people die. Sometime I drove my car at freeway in the
                                              vt
holiday. I was careful because some driver drank alcohol to celebrate the

holiday. Even the police and highway partol couldn't stop them. When

they drank alot of beer, they couldn't control their car. Then they
                                                        modal (vt)
would hit some car in the front of them or rear. So the car passager <u>will</u>
            modal (vt)
be a victim. They <u>may</u> lose their life. If I didn't have a car, I would   *What do*
                                                                              you mean
travel around the United State.   *here?*

   In conclusion, I will give some advice to the car owners. [They will
         unclear
know the car which is cost them a lot.] They can't become a drunk

driver.

End Comment:

   Although you have some good ideas about problems with cars, the
   major weakness is that the essay does not focus on the question. Your
   paper deals with your own personal experiences with a car rather than
   on the more general idea of a "technological development."
   If you choose to rewrite this paper, be especially aware of problems
   with verb tense, verb form, and focus.

PART 2:

How the Instructor Can
Help Students Learn to Do
Error Analysis

■ CHAPTER 6: Helping Students Work on Their Sentence Errors

In the chapters in Part One, you learned how to respond to the content and sentence-level features of ESL compositions. In Part Two, you will learn how to help students use the feedback you have given them on sentences, specifically by helping them implement a systematic approach to error analysis. This systematic approach to error analysis will be a discovery process for the students in which they become aware of their most serious and frequent sentence errors, decide which errors to work on first, and then learn problem-solving strategies for correcting their errors. The end goal of this whole system of error analysis is to enable students to develop independent self-monitoring skills so that they can correct sentence errors on their own. As you read this chapter, you may choose to read the theory/background sections, which will give you more details on the theory of error analysis and language acquisition.

In helping students learn a systematic approach to error analysis, moving from identification to eventual self-correction and reduction of errors, you can choose, according to your time constraints, whether to locate and identify sentence-level errors only or to work collaboratively with the student after error identification. With either method—the student working independently or collaborating with the instructor—you will help the student move toward independent self-monitoring, the end goal of the entire process of error analysis.

If you only give feedback on errors, such as identifying them with the grading symbols you learned in Chapter 3, you will thus be giving the student complete responsibility beyond identification for working on his or her sentence errors. If, on the other hand, you help the student implement the following error analysis system, you can choose to what extent you wish to collaborate with the student to help the student:

1. determine his or her most serious and frequent systematic sentence errors

2. decide which sentence errors to work on first

3. develop problem-solving strategies for working on these errors

4. become an independent self-monitor of his or her errors.

In the sections below, you will learn the four steps in the error analysis process and will be given different options you may choose from to tailor the system to your own needs.

> **Step 1:** *Helping the Student Determine His or Her Most Serious and Frequent Sentence Errors*
>
> **Step 2:** *Helping the Student Learn How to Prioritize His or Her Sentence Errors and Set Realistic Goals for Working on Them*
>
> **Step 3:** *Helping the Student Learn Problem-Solving Strategies for Working on His or Her Sentence Errors*
>
> **Step 4:** *Moving the Student Into Independent Self-Monitoring*

Step 1:   Helping the Student Determine His or Her Most Serious and Frequent Errors

As part of the whole discovery process in this error analysis system, the student will first need to determine what his or her most serious and frequent errors are. In this step, the instructor, who has already given the student valuable feedback on his or her sentence errors by locating and identifying them when reading the paper, has two options: to collaborate fully with the student or, as much as possible, have the student work on his or her own. The instructor can decide how much assistance to give the student depending on the instructor's time constraints, the student's motivation, and the student's level of proficiency.

An integral part of error analysis is tallying sentence errors, either formally by recording errors or informally by mentally keeping track of them. A very helpful device for recording errors is some type of tally sheet. The Error Awareness Sheet* is a tally sheet designed to help students discover what their most serious and frequent sentence errors are and to determine the order in which they should work on these errors. It is keyed to the grading symbols in Chapter 3 and divided into global and local errors. Also listed are ten errors native speakers commonly make that are not included in the system but that the instructor may wish to mark, such as pronoun reference or sentence fragments. Instead of formally recording errors, the instructor may, of course, decide to use an informal method of tallying errors, such as mentally keeping track of them while marking a paper and then indicating to the student in an end comment what his or her most serious and frequent errors are. Both these methods of tallying are further explained in this chapter.

---

*Lalande (1982) used the term Error Awareness Sheet for the tally sheet he used in his study.

▼ **Background/Theory:** Research on error analysis and language acquisition suggests that tally sheets or checklists are helpful tools for teachers to record language errors (Hendrickson 1980a,b; Lalande 1982; and Walz 1982). This research suggests that the information recorded on tally sheets is useful for instructors to diagnose students' errors and to make decisions about teaching error correction. Lalande developed what he termed an Error Awareness Sheet as part of a study in which he found that intermediate students of German could improve their writing when they were made aware of their errors through identification by symbols and made aware of the frequency of their errors through a tally sheet. Students subsequently corrected their errors using problem-solving techniques such as consulting a grammar review text (Lalande 1982).

Options for Helping the Student Determine His or Her Most Serious and Frequent Errors

You will find the following options useful to consider in deciding how large a role you want to play as you move the student into learning what his or her most serious and frequent errors are. In Options A and B, the instructor is more involved than in C and D, which are more student-centered.

Option A —You can tally the errors *informally* by getting an overall sense of them as you read the paper and then indicate to the student his or her most serious and frequent errors in an end comment.

If you selectively mark a paper for its most serious and frequent errors, you will be mentally keeping track of the sentence errors, but will not actually be counting or totaling them. For example, in the first two paragraphs of a paper, you might notice that the student is making errors with verb tense, verb form, connectors, number, and word choice and decide to mark the paper selectively for these errors. Then, in the end comment, you could tell the student that these are his or her most serious and frequent errors.

If, on the other hand, you are working with a high-level, very motivated student and decide to mark most of the errors in a paper rather than selectively mark them, you will most probably scan the paper to get an overall sense of the student's most serious and frequent errors and give the student feedback on these errors in an end comment, saying, for example, "I noticed that you were making frequent global errors with the conditional and modals and with sub-ject–verb agreement (a local error)."

If you choose Option A, you must remember that you, instead of the student, are taking responsibility for determining the student's most serious and frequent errors. The student is not yet entering directly into the discovery process.

Option B — You can tally the errors *formally* by using a tally sheet such as the "Error Awareness Sheet" on p. 90.

Instead of informally tallying the errors while marking the paper, you could, after identifying them in the paper, use a tally sheet such as the Error Awareness Sheet. As you can see in the sample Error Awareness Sheet on p. 91 that has been filled in, you would put a check for each error you marked in the paper in the "Total Number of Errors" column. You will fill in the column "Top Priority Errors to Work On" in Step 2.

If you choose to fill out this kind of Error Awareness Sheet, you are assuming the responsibility for determining the student's most serious and frequent errors and the student is not yet entering into the process of discovering his or her most serious and frequent sentence errors. However, if you want your students to participate in this initial stage of the discovery process but still feel they need guidance, you could, the first time, fill in the tally sheet as an example, or you could enter only those errors identified in the first two paragraphs to show the student how to use the Error Awareness Sheet and then let the student finish filling in the Error Awareness Sheet.

Option C — You can encourage the student to tally his or her own errors by filling out the Error Awareness Sheet in class individually or with a peer, outside of class, or with the help of a tutor in a tutoring session.

In this option, the student is directly entering into the discovery process by actively participating in determining his or her most serious and frequent errors. Moreover, this participation helps the student see the grading symbols as part of a larger error analysis process and not just as marks that designate errors.

Depending on when you want the student to begin the process of learning the error analysis system, you may choose to have the student fill out the Error Awareness Sheet starting with the first essay or wait until you have marked several pieces of the student's writing. In the latter case, the student can tally the errors from the accumulated pieces of writing all together on one Error

Awareness Sheet. When the student hands in his or her next essay, it is often useful to have the student attach the Error Awareness Sheet from his or her last essay to it so that you have a visual record of the student's pattern of errors from the previous essay and do not have to resort to your memory.

In having the students fill in the Error Awareness Sheet on their own, you need to keep in mind that the lower level student will most likely need more assistance in completing the Error Awareness Sheet than a higher level student, particularly if you have elected to mark many errors.

Option D—You and the student together can fill out the "Error Awareness Sheet" in a conference.

In this option, you and the student would fill out the Error Awareness Sheet together in a conference either during class or outside of class. While this procedure can be very time-consuming, particularly if you are teaching several writing classes, it might be an effective way to get the student started on the whole process of learning to analyze his or her sentence errors so that he or she can then fill out subsequent Error Awareness Sheets independently.

The Error Awareness Sheet: Purpose, Benefits of, and Samples

The Error Awareness Sheet serves two purposes: to help the student discover the most serious and frequent errors in his or her writing and prioritize those errors in order to know which errors to begin working on. An especially helpful visual aid for the student, it can start a student moving quickly into the error analysis process. Moreover, because it provides a written record of the student's errors, the student knows, before the next essay, what errors he or she is making and can start editing for them. The student can then see from essay to essay just how much progress he or she is making in reducing errors.

Seeing a written record that proves his or her sentence errors are decreasing helps a student feel more motivated to continue working on sentence-level errors. However, for some students, seeing the number of errors they are making can be overwhelming and depressing, but such a record may be a necessary jolt to move them away from sentence-level errors and towards sentence accuracy.

Two sample Error Awareness Sheets follow: one is blank and the other is an example of a filled-in tally sheet.

Error Awareness Sheet

Directions: This Error Awareness Sheet will help you to discover what your sentence-level errors are and to learn to prioritize them. Put a check in the second column for each error marked on your returned paper. Then, from the most frequent errors in the second column, select two or three that you can begin working on first and put a check next to them in the third column. Always remember that you need to work on frequent global errors first.

Name of Student: **Essay:**

TYPE OF ERROR	TOTAL NUMBER OF ERRORS	TOP-PRIORITY ERRORS TO WORK ON
GLOBAL ERRORS (more serious)		
vt		
vf		
modal		
cond		
ss		
wo		
conn		
pass		
unclear		
LOCAL ERRORS (less serious)		
sv		
art		
num		
wc		
wf		
nonidiom		
OTHER ERRORS		
cap		
coh		
cs		
dm		
frag		
lc		
p		
pro ref/agree		
ro		
sp		

Error Awareness Sheet

Directions: This Error Awareness Sheet will help you to discover what your sentence-level errors are and to learn to prioritize them. Put a check in the second column for each error marked on your returned paper. Then, from the most frequent errors in the second column, select two or three that you can begin working on first and put a check next to them in the third column. Always remember that you need to work on frequent global errors first.

Name of Student: **Essay:**

TYPE OF ERROR	TOTAL NUMBER OF ERRORS	TOP-PRIORITY ERRORS TO WORK ON
GLOBAL ERRORS (more serious)		
vt	✓✓✓✓✓✓	✓
vf		
modal	✓✓✓✓	✓
cond		
ss		
wo	✓✓✓✓✓✓✓	✓
conn	✓✓	
pass		
unclear		
LOCAL ERRORS (less serious)		
sv		
art	✓✓✓✓✓✓✓✓✓✓✓	✓
num	✓✓✓✓✓✓✓✓	✓
wc	✓✓	
wf		
nonidiom	✓✓✓✓	
OTHER ERRORS		
cap		
coh		
cs	✓✓	
dm		
frag		
lc		
p		
pro ref/agree	✓	
ro		
sp		

Step 2:   Helping the Student Learn How to Prioritize His or Her Sentence Errors and Set Realistic Goals for Working on Them

Once the student, working on his or her own or in collaboration with the instructor or a tutor, has determined his or her most serious and frequent errors, the student is ready to learn the next step in the error analysis system: how to prioritize sentence errors, that is, to decide which sentence errors to work on first. In this step, just as in the previous one, the instructor can choose to collaborate with the student or to have the student work alone or with a tutor depending on time constraints, the student's level of proficiency, or other factors such as whether the class is made up of strictly ESL writers.

The student needs to accomplish two things in this step of the error analysis system:

* decide which sentence errors need immediate attention

* set realistic goals for working on these errors

If, in Step 1, for example, the student has determined he or she is making frequent errors with sentence structure, modals, and verb tense (global errors) as well as with subject–verb agreement and number (local errors), the student now needs to discover which error(s) from that list to work on first because it would be unrealistic to work on all of them at once.

The student should usually be advised to give his or her most frequent global errors the highest priority unless a local error is so frequent that it needs attention immediately. A feasible plan would be for the student to select two or three of the top-priority errors to work on first and then as he or she begins to control these errors, to move on to the other top-priority errors, and then eventually to less serious and frequent errors. Of course, a high-level, highly motivated student could work on both global and local errors and tackle more errors than the less proficient or less motivated student. As the student continues to get feedback on his or her sentence errors in returned essays and drafts, the student will, of course, have to be flexible in prioritizing errors, adding an error that has become more frequent to the errors that he or she is working on or temporarily abandoning an error in favor of another error that has suddenly become more serious. Also, sometimes, even though you would prefer that the student work on other errors, the student might want to start work on a "favorite" error. For example, if a student is certain that article errors are his or her most important error, it might be a good idea to have the student start with this error instead of his or her errors with verb tense and sentence structure so that he or she will be more psychologically willing to proceed to the errors that he or she really needs to work on. Alternatively, you could suggest to the student that he or she work on the "favorite" error along with his or her most serious and frequent errors.

As well as setting up an order in which to work on errors, the student needs to set realistic goals. First of all, the student needs to understand that total sentence accuracy is not very realistic, but reduction of errors is. Secondly, the student needs to be aware that understanding an error takes time and that reducing its occurrence in his or her writing can be a slow process, especially if the error is fossilized. Therefore, the student needs to decide how long he or she should spend working on the errors he or she has selected to work on first before continuing on to other errors that need attention. The student might set a goal to first fully understand what the error is, begin correcting for it, and then to continue on to the next error. Above all, the student must learn to be flexible and not get stuck on certain errors and neglect others that need attention.

You will find the following options useful in deciding how large a role you want to play in helping the student determine which errors to work on first and to set goals for working on these errors.

Options for Helping the Student Learn How to Prioritize His or Her Sentence Errors and Set Realistic Goals for Working on Them

Option A—The instructor assumes the responsibility of deciding for the student which sentence errors need immediate attention and sets goals for the student.

In this option, the instructor indicates, in the end comment of the paper or in the third column of the Error Awareness Sheet, "Top Priority Errors to Work on"—or both—what errors the student needs to work on first. For example, the instructor could say in an end comment: "Although you are making frequent global errors with verb tense, verb form, and connectors, as well as with the local errors article and word choice (especially prepositions), it would be best if you began working on verb tense and connectors immediately."

Although in this option you are not actively involving the student in setting priorities for working on his or her sentence errors, you are still helping the student significantly in starting the discovery process of error analysis because even a short note in an end comment directing the student to work on two or three global errors can be a help, especially to students at a lower level of proficiency who may feel they have little control over their errors and do not know where to start working on them. You might elect, alternatively, to help the student set priorities after the first paper and then give the student the responsibility of deciding which errors to work on first in subsequent papers.

Option B—The student assumes the responsibility of deciding which errors to work on first.

After either the student or you have filled out the Error Awareness Sheet, the student then decides which errors he or she needs to work on first. Many students will have problems with this decision because they believe they should be working on all their errors at once. Thus, if you choose this option and if you are teaching an ESL composition class, it might be practical for you to discuss this step in class or briefly go around the class checking the students' filled-in Error Awareness Sheets to check what errors students have marked as their top priority. (If the ESL student is in a mainstream composition class, you could suggest a brief conference during office hours.) For example, you might suggest to students that they select two to four errors to work on first, cautioning them to pick those two to four from their most serious and frequent errors. Even though the instructor may have to enter into the process to clarify how to decide which errors to start working on, the student is still very actively involved in the discovery process.

What is most important is that the students themselves discover that there is a hierarchy of errors, that some errors affect communication more than others, and that the grading symbols have a broader function than merely locating and identifying an error in a sentence.

Option C—The student can collaborate with the instructor or with a tutor to determine which errors to work on first.

Instead of making all the decisions independently, the student could collaborate with the instructor in an in-class conference or during office hours or, alternatively, work with a tutor. Given the limited time of most composition instructors, you would probably not be able to spend an inordinate amount of time setting goals with a student in conference. However, at least for the first paper, this option might prove very useful. Then, in subsequent papers, as the student has entered more fully into the error analysis system, he or she could just ask questions if he or she is having problems deciding which errors to work on.

Step 3:   Helping the Student Learn Problem-Solving Strategies for Working on His or Her Sentence Errors

Once the student has identified his or her most serious and frequent sentence errors, has prioritized them, and has set goals for working on these errors, he or she is then ready to learn problem-solving strategies for working on these sentence-level errors. In this step, the student should work as independently as possible.

The problem-solving strategies that the student will need to learn are:

Step 3A: Understanding What the Error Is

Step 3B: Correcting the Error

Step 3C: Determining the Cause of the Error, If Possible

Step 3A: Understanding What the Error Is

When you mark the student's paper, you locate and identify the error. Then the student needs to discover exactly what type of error he or she is making because in this error analysis system, which is based on discovery, the error has not been corrected. For example, an error with verb tense could indicate a problem using any one of the tenses or an inappropriate shifting of tenses. Similarly, an error with sentence structure might be omitting the verb *to be* as in *I happy* or doubling the subject as in *My friends and I we like ice cream.* If a student can discover exactly what aspects of the error he or she needs to control, the student will increase his or her chance of reducing that error in writing.

Although students can consult an ESL grammar book to study the error or find certain answers in an ESL dictionary, those methods will not be as efficient as using this book's companion text, *Writing Clearly: An Editing Guide,* which has been expressly written to accompany this book and is specifically geared toward grammar in the context of formal writing. In fact, if the instructor is using the grading symbols and error analysis system in this book, ideally students in an ESL writing course would be using *Writing Clearly* as a text, or the ESL student in a composition class for native speakers would be using it as a supplemental text, since handbooks written for mainstream composition classes treat ESL errors briefly, if at all.

Each unit in *Writing Clearly: An Editing Guide* is keyed to the grading symbols that were presented in Chapter 3. Each unit covers one of the 15 errors, listing the most common problems ESL students have with this particular error in writing and illustrating each problem with selected grammar rules and self-help strategies, all of which furnish the student with the background he or she needs to understand the error and to consciously control it. The student is directed to study each problem and the examples that illustrate it and then mark the problems he or she has with that particular error when writing in English. For example, in the unit on word choice, the student can discover whether his or her problems are, for example, with choosing the wrong preposition or using a word that does not exist. As part of the process of learning to be independent and discovering answers on his or her own, the student is sometimes directed to an ESL dictionary to verify a verb + preposition combination, for example, or to an ESL grammar text to study a fine point of grammar. The student is also encouraged to improve his or her writing skills independently through reading or asking a native speaker for clarification. By going through the discovery process outlined in *Writing Clearly,* the student should be able to discover exactly what type of error he or she is making.

Writing Clearly: An Editing Guide offers, in each unit, a definition of the error, a discussion of why it is important to master it, and suggested strategies for mastering the error. Each unit also has exercises to help students test their ability to identify and correct the error and writing topics that can be assigned.

If you are using *Writing Clearly: An Editing Guide* as a text in an ESL writing course, you might teach the units selectively, according to what your students' needs are. Yet even if you decide to cover all the units in the book, a student could still use a unit that has not yet been taught in order to discover his or her particular error. Remember that *Writing Clearly,* although written for students, can also serve as a reference text for the instructor because it gives a full explanation of the grading symbols presented in Chapter 3. Furthermore, it is a good reference tool for instructors who are not familiar with ESL errors.

Once a student has discovered exactly what his or her errors are and understands the errors, he or she is ready for the next step in the process of error analysis: correcting sentences with these errors.

Step 3B: Correcting the Error

As part of the error analysis process, students need to correct their sentence errors after they have discovered what these errors are. However, instead of simply correcting a single word or phrase, the student needs to revise, at a minimum, whole sentences. In fact, research suggests that rather than just correcting the error itself, students benefit from revising complete sentences, paragraphs, or whole papers (Friedman 1983).

Because of time constraints, however, you may want to encourage selective revising of a small number of sentences or selected paragraphs. For example, you might direct the student to do the following:

- to revise several sentences in which his or her most serious and frequent errors occur. Although you might perhaps identify these sentences by a star or an asterisk on the student's paper, the student can just as easily select several sentences to correct, based on the knowledge he or she has from determining his or her most serious and frequent sentence errors.

- to revise one paragraph with, for example, several of the student's predominant problems, such as inappropriate shifting of verb tense, several errors with the conditional, and numerous errors with articles

- to revise all sentences containing a certain type of error

- to revise for an error recently taught in class

When the student has revised the sentences on his or her own, you can choose either to look at them yourself or have the student work with a tutor.

> **▼ Background/Theory:** Several researchers have suggested that students can also profit from working on error correction with their peers (Witbeck 1976; Hendrickson 1980a; Walz 1982; Lalande 1982).

Step 3C: Determining the Cause of the Error, If Possible

Research suggests that students will benefit from determining the underlying causes of their sentence errors whenever it is possible to explain them (Kroll and Schafer 1978; Xu 1989; Raimes 1991). Once the student understands the reason behind the error (that the error results either from a transfer of rules from his or her native language or from a hypothesis about the new language that he or she is testing), he or she might more readily accept that the error signals progress in gaining second language proficiency because it is part of the process of language acquisition. The student will then often be more willing and able to correct the error.

Yet for even the most experienced ESL instructor, a complete analysis of the underlying causes of error can be difficult. However, even the most rudimentary discussion of causes, whether in class, in a conference, or even in an end comment, can be helpful to the student. For example, you might tell the student that one of the reasons he or she is having difficulty with verb tenses is that they do not exist in his or her native language or that *My roommate can draws very well* is an overgeneralization of the third person singular in the present tense. It has also been suggested that having students hypothesize why they are making a particular error helps them enter into thinking about the importance of sentence accuracy (Kroll and Schafer 1978; Raimes 1991).

▼ **Background/Theory:** The underlying causes of error can be either *interlingual,* the transfer of rules from the student's native language, or *intralingual,* the simplification or overgeneralization of rules within the second language (Selinker 1974; Kroll and Schafer 1978; Raimes 1991). In both cases, the student is forming hypotheses about the structure of English, hypotheses based on the rules of his or her native language or hypotheses based on a rule of English that he or she has learned and is over-applying.

Interlingual Example:

Because most Asian languages do not signal tense within the verb, students who speak these Asian languages have a great deal of difficulty mastering the complex English verb tense system. In the sentence *Last night it rain,* the student applies the rule from his or her own language that *last night* signals the past and that putting the verb in the past is not necessary.

Intralingual Example:

Over generalization of rules:

The student learns that 3rd person singular verbs end in *-s.*

   Example: *She walks to school.*

The student overgeneralizes and uses *-s* inappropriately with the verb in a modal verb phrase.

   Incorrect: *She can walks to school.*

Step 4: Moving the Student Into Independent Self-Monitoring

Once the student has learned the error analysis system, he or she is ready to become an independent user of it. The whole discovery process of error analysis that the student has been learning is directed towards the student's building up a *self-monitor* that he or she can use in independent editing; that is, ideally the student independently senses and corrects errors at some point during the writing process, either while composing or in revising drafts.

While most second language learners benefit from using the self-monitor, you will need to caution students against over-monitoring or under-monitoring and may want to make suggestions to the student that will guide him or her in developing an effective self-monitor.

▼ **Background/Theory:** See Krashen 1981 and 1982 for a discussion of the Monitor Theory and problems second language learners have with using the monitor.

Problems With Using the Monitor

Even though the research is not yet conclusive and a model for ideal self-monitoring use has not yet been agreed upon, instructors can help students with problems they are having in using a self-monitor. Keep in mind that use of the self-monitor varies significantly from student to student according to individual learning styles. Some problems that students may have with self-monitoring are that students may have no self-monitor or an underdeveloped self-monitor, while others might have an over-developed self-monitor.

Problems with Under-Monitoring

Some students may have developed no self-monitor and might not be able to recognize errors they are making while composing or revising. Others may decide to focus entirely on content (choosing not to use the sentence-level monitor) when writing under time pressure, assuming that they will have time to clean up sentence errors in the proofreading stage. Such under-monitoring, however, is not realistic for most ESL students.

For the student who under-monitors, you can suggest the importance of the student's watching for his or her two to four most serious and frequent errors during the writing process, especially when writing under time pressure.

Problems with Over-Monitoring

Students who focus primarily on form, not content, as they write may find the flow of their ideas blocked and thus their fluency is affected (Krashen 1982; Jones 1985). An over-user might stop very frequently to check and/or rewrite many words or phrases while composing. You can suggest to the student who over-monitors that he or she only monitor for his or her most serious and frequent errors so that he or she can remain focused on content rather than pondering over each word he or she produces in a sentence. The student can then shift his or her primary focus to content so that he or she can then produce a logical train of ideas. While revising a draft, the student could then monitor for other errors.

Most importantly, instructors can share with all ESL students that although self-monitoring can be helpful, it is not beneficial when it interferes with the communication process.

▼ **Background/Theory:** Researchers have not yet determined when the monitor is most effectively used in the writing process (Zamel 1983; Raimes 1985; Silva 1989; Krappels 1990). While research into the writing process of native speakers indicates that ideally the writer should focus more on content than on form in the early stages of writing, research into the ESL writing process has not yet indicated either when in the writing process ESL writers actually use the monitor or when the monitor is most effective (before, during, or after producing a sentence, or after producing an entire draft). Thus, research into the ESL writing process is in its early stages and is not yet conclusive in terms of the most effective use of the self-monitor.

Conclusion

In using a systematic approach to error analysis, instructors are helping students learn to analyze their specific sentence-level weaknesses and develop strategies for improving their sentence-level control when they write. In helping students move toward independent self-monitoring, the goal of the entire error analysis process, the instructor is putting students in a much stronger position to take on the challenges of writing in the academic and professional worlds.

APPENDIX

Developing Written Grading Standards

Many composition instructors find it particularly useful to use a set of written grading standards to help them determine grades on papers and to help them grade as consistently as possible. This section, which is divided into the three parts listed below, will give you guidance on how to develop written grading standards for yourself or for your program.

> **Part 1:** *Grading Standards—What Are They?*
> **Part 2:** *Some Useful Guidelines for Developing Grading Standards*
> **Part 3:** *Three Sets of Sample Grading Standards*

Part 1: Grading Standards—What Are They?

Grading standards, also called *grading rubrics* or *scoring guides,* provide instructors and exam graders with a description of the distinguishing characteristics of "A" through "F" papers or of passing versus failing papers on a placement exam or exit exam. Such written grading standards have a paragraph describing papers that fall into each level or category (see Sample Grading Standards I through III in Part 3 of this appendix).

Grading standards provide you with criteria to use in assigning grades to ESL papers. Furthermore, written grading standards adopted by a program encourage standardization of grading so that instructors assign grades as uniformly as possible within a program. Written grading standards also give students not only a clear picture of the writing standards they are expected to achieve, but also the sense that grades are being assigned fairly and consistently in the class and/or in the writing program.

You may already be in a situation, such as in a college or university composition program, where instructors rely heavily on the written grading standards developed for the program. Yet, if your program does not have written grading standards and you are expected to determine your own grading criteria, you will find it helpful to develop an informal set of written grading standards for your own use.

Whether you alone or you along with a committee of instructors or a program administrator decide to develop a set of written grading standards, you will need to determine how these standards will be used. For instance, will you need different standards for each level of your program, or can one set of standards be applied at all levels? Will you be using these standards to place students into your program, to grade their essays during the term, and/or to determine whether they are ready to move on to the next level?

Before developing your own standards, you may also want to look at standards already developed by others, such as those in Part 3 of this appendix. You might also contact program administrators to ask to see their grading standards. Standards from other programs would, of course, need to be adapted for use in your classroom and program.

Part 2:   Guidelines for Developing Grading Standards

As you write grading standards for yourself or your program, keep the following five guidelines in mind:

I. Indicate the dominant characteristic of a paper in each category.

Be certain that you indicate, preferably at the beginning of the description of each category, the dominant characteristic of papers in that category. This dominant characteristic might be set apart in a separate sentence or phrase at the beginning of the description of a category. For example, the description of the "A" paper in Sample Grading Standards I begins with the dominant characteristic of papers in that category: "Papers in this category show strong control of organization, development, and language." Alternatively, the dominant characteristic may appear in key words in the first sentence at the beginning of the descriptive paragraph of a category. In Sample Grading Standards III, the key words for a "6" paper are "commands attention," while the key words for a "2" paper are "shows serious weaknesses."

2. Organize the standards so that they progress from an outstanding down to a weak paper.

You will find it most helpful to begin the grading standards with a description of the highest category—an outstanding paper. Then describe how papers in each category weaken as they drop away from the standard of the outstanding paper.

3. Include organization, development, and sentence-level features in each description.

The standards should cover expectations for all aspects of a good piece of writing, typically organization, development, and sentences. Descriptive coverage of these three areas gives the message that a paper should not be judged on one aspect alone, such as sentence-level errors.

For clear examples of how grading standards should cover all the aspects of good writing, see the description of a "6" paper in Sample Grading Standards III or that of an "A" paper in Sample Grading Standards I.

4. Aim for a balance between general and specific description.

In each category, you should describe strengths and/or weaknesses of typical papers at that level. Detailed descriptions are very helpful for some instructors, especially new composition teachers, but too much detail will overwhelm both the instructors and the students who are using the standards. You will, however, need to be certain that your descriptions clearly distinguish between the two categories at the pass/fail line, if there is such a line. Thus, in these two categories, more detailed description may be needed to make clear why a paper would fall either above or below the passing line.

5. Aim for clarity, above all.

In writing the description of each category, your overall goal is to make certain that instructors and students can see what is expected of papers that fall into the different categories. When the written grading standards are clear in this way, they are particularly helpful for an instructor to discuss in class along with sample graded papers that illustrate one or more of the categories. Most importantly, the standards need to be clear enough for instructors to apply them and for students to understand them.

Part 3: Sample Grading Standards

Three sets of sample grading standards are found in this section. While each of these sets of standards was developed for a different purpose, all three illustrate the guidelines outlined above.

Sample Grading Standards I and II were developed for use in undergraduate ESL composition classes at the University of California, Davis. These classes precede basic writing and freshman composition classes at the university.

Sample Grading Standards **I** is used to determine grades on essays written during the term and to guide the instructor in assigning "A" through "F" grades on papers based on the papers' dominant characteristics. These particular standards, used for all three levels of an ESL composition program, are quite demanding, reflecting the high standards of a university-level composition program.

Sample Grading Standards **II** illustrates grading criteria for the final exam in the same ESL program. This rather extensive set of standards includes a separate set of criteria for each level of the program—Beginning ESL Composition (English 21), Intermediate ESL Composition (English 22), and Advanced ESL Composition (English 23). Because the final exam is an exit exam, the standards include more detail on sentence-level control expected at each class level and within each category.

Sample Grading Standards **III** (taken from Gadda 1992) has been developed and used by the University of California in the grading of its universitywide (nine-campus) Subject A Examination. This exam is taken by entering freshmen to determine whether or not they need to take a basic writing course before taking freshman English. The standards of this scoring guide are applied in evaluating all papers, including ESL papers.

SAMPLE GRADING STANDARDS I

University of California, Davis
English for Nonnative Speakers Undergraduate Program

English 21, 22, and 23 Grading Standards

Excellent — "A"

Papers in this category show *strong control of organization, development, and language.*

Organization:

Thesis is clear, and paragraph topics are clearly stated and related to the thesis, with each paragraph leading clearly and logically to the next. The introduction is well developed and engages the reader's interest, and the conclusion does more than summarize.

Development:

The main point of each paragraph is developed through analysis, detail, and example. The paper has a good balance between generalizations and specifics and flows coherently. If based on a reading passage, the paper shows good comprehension of the reading passage.

Grammar and Mechanics:

The paper contains few sentence-level errors. The writer uses a variety of sentence types effectively.

Vocabulary:

Word choice is precise, and usage is accurate. Idioms are controlled. The writer shows an awareness of word connotations and a control of formal written English.

Good — "B"

Papers in this category show *good control of essay organization and development but contain some errors in language which do not impede understanding of the writer's ideas.*

These papers have a clear thesis which is well supported, though certain points may be weak in evidence or analysis. The papers have generally good coherence. Introduction or conclusion may contain weaknesses. Language is generally fluent, and most errors in grammar or mechanics are non-disruptive, such as those involving number, articles, prepositions, pronoun reference, or subject–verb agreement. Use of verbs is largely controlled, although a few verb tense and/or verb form errors may occur. Some nonidiomatic language and some inaccuracies in word choice may occur. If based on a reading passage, the paper shows an accurate understanding of the reading passage.

Adequate — "C"

Papers in this category show *adequate control of essay organization and development, but contain more errors in language than a "B" paper.* These errors, however, do not dominate the paper.

These papers are organized around a central idea, although the thesis may be weak and support is generally weaker than that of a "B" paper. At least a minimum of evidence and analysis is presented for each point, but one or more of the following may occur: weak analysis, some overdependence on narration or summary, some coherence problems. Errors in grammar, word order, or mechanics may include non-disruptive and some disruptive errors. (Errors that can be disruptive include: verb tense and form, sentence structure, predication, inaccuracies in word choice or form.) Sentences should show some variety, with few fragments or run-ons. There are few unclear sentences. If the paper is based on a reading passage, slight inaccuracies in comprehension of the reading passage may occur.

Poor — "D"

Papers in this category show *poor control of essay organization, development, and/or language.*

These papers may have no clear thesis or may not address the essay question. They may contain serious weaknesses in evidence and/or analysis or serious and repeated coherence problems. Serious and frequent disruptive errors may dominate the paper. The paper may show heavy reliance on simple sentences, exhibit a noticeably limited vocabulary, or contain frequent unclear sentences. If based on a reading passage, the paper may show misunderstanding of the reading passage.

Failing — "F"

A paper may be given an "F" if it completely lacks a controlling idea, is totally incomprehensible at the sentence level, is off topic, or extremely brief. Generally, however, a paper which is submitted on time and which attempts to address the topic will receive a grade of at least "D–."

NOTE: SERIOUS FLAWS IN ANY ONE AREA (ORGANIZATION, DEVELOPMENT, OR SENTENCES) WILL PULL DOWN THE GRADE OF AN OTHERWISE STRONG PAPER.

SAMPLE GRADING STANDARDS II

University of California, Davis

English for Nonnative Speakers Undergraduate Program

Final Exam Grading Standards

English 23 — Analytical Essay Based on a Reading Passage

P **Pass** (competent paper)

Organization:

Development:

Language:

Development

A clearly stated thesis responding to the question.

Clear paragraph topics related to the thesis.

An introduction leading to the thesis, and a conclusion.

Control of transitions and other coherence devices.

Unified, coherent paragraphs focused on the question.

Specific appropriate support from the reading passage and, if appropriate, personal experience.

Logical analysis showing accurate understanding of the reading passage.

May include minor lapses in development.

Scattered errors which generally do not impede understanding.

Good control of sentence structure and boundaries plus sentence variety.

Good control of verbs: formation, agreement, and tenses, and some control of the conditional.

General control of number, articles, and pronoun consistency.

Vocabulary: variety and accuracy in word choice; generally correct word formation.

P– **Marginal Pass** (adequate paper)

Organization:

A thesis responding to the question.

One or more paragraph topics may be ineffectively stated.

Introduction and perhaps minimal conclusion.

Some appropriate transitions and other coherence devices.

Generally unified and coherent paragraphs focused on the question.

Some generalizations may not be adequately supported; some use of the reading passage may be ineffective.

Analysis is generally logical and shows understanding of the reading passage.

Language:

An accumulation of errors which may occasionally impede understanding.

General control of sentence structure and boundaries plus sentence variety.

General control of verbs: formation, agreement, and tenses.

Some control of number, articles, and pronoun consistency.

Vocabulary: variety in word choice; adequate control of word formation.

NP+ Marginal Fail (inadequate paper weak in one or more of the following three categories)

Organization:

Unclear or faulty thesis.

Topics of one or more paragraphs unclear or unrelated to thesis.

Transitions missing or generally incorrect.

Development:

Serious coherence problems in one or more paragraphs.

Inadequate support which may veer seriously off topic, noticeably lack specifics, or distort the meaning of the reading passage.

Analysis lacking, not logical, or not focused on the question.

Language:

Frequent errors which often impede understanding.

Problems in sentence structure and boundaries; little use of subordination.

Problems with many verbs: formation, agreement, tenses.

Much inaccuracy in word choice and word forms.

NP Clear Fail (very weak paper showing that the writer should not proceed to the next level)

NOTE: NORMALLY THE NP GRADE REFLECTS DEFICIENCIES IN LANGUAGE, NOT IN ORGANIZATION AND/OR DEVELOPMENT. IN RARE CASES, HOWEVER, A PAPER WITH SEVERE ORGANIZATION OR DEVELOPMENT PROBLEMS CAN RECEIVE AN NP.

Language:

Paper dominated by major and repeated errors (disruptive and nondisruptive).

Many unclear sentences.

Lack of control of sentence structure and many verbs.

Noticeably limited vocabulary.

Noticeable inability to clearly express complex ideas.

SAMPLE GRADING STANDARDS II

University of California, Davis
English for Nonnative Speakers Undergraduate Program

Final Exam Grading Standards

English 22 — 4- or 5-Paragraph Expository Essay Based on Personal Experience

P   Pass   (competent paper)

Organization:

A clearly stated thesis responding to the question.

Topic sentences in each paragraph which are related to the thesis.

An introduction leading to the thesis, and a conclusion.

Appropriate transitions and other coherence devices.

Development:

Unified, coherent paragraphs focused on the question.

Specific, appropriate support and logical analysis.

May include minor lapses in development.

Language:

Scattered errors which generally do not impede understanding.

Adequate control of sentence structure and boundaries plus sentence variety.

Adequate control of verbs: formation, agreement, tenses.

Some control of number, articles, and pronouns.

Vocabulary: variety and accuracy in word choice; generally correct word formation.

P–   Marginal Pass   (adequate paper)

Organization:

A thesis responding to the question.

An attempt at topic sentences.

Introduction and perhaps minimal conclusion.

Some appropriate transitions and other coherence devices.

Development

Generally unified and coherent paragraphs focused on the question.

Specific support and some attempt at logical analysis.

Language:

An accumulation of errors which sometimes impede understanding.

Minimally adequate control of sentence structure and boundaries plus sentence variety.

Minimally adequate control of verbs: formation, agreement, tenses.

Some control of number, articles, and pronouns.

Vocabulary: variety in word choice and some control of word formation.

NP+   Marginal Fail (inadequate paper weak in one or more of the following three categories)

Organization:

Unclear or faulty thesis.

Topics of one or more paragraphs unclear or unrelated to thesis.

Transitions missing or generally incorrect.

Development:

Serious coherence problems in one or more paragraphs.

Inadequate support which may veer seriously off topic or noticeably lack specifics.

Analysis lacking, not logical, or not focused on the question.

Language:

Frequent errors which often impede understanding.

Problems in sentence structure and boundaries; little use of subordination.

Problems with many verbs: formation, agreement, tenses.

Much inaccuracy in word choice and word formation.

NP   Clear Fail   (very weak paper showing that the writer should not proceed to the next level)

NOTE: NORMALLY THE NP GRADE REFLECTS DEFICIENCIES IN LANGUAGE, NOT IN ORGANIZATION AND/OR DEVELOPMENT. IN RARE CASES, HOWEVER, A PAPER WITH SEVERE ORGANIZATION OR DEVELOPMENT PROBLEMS CAN RECEIVE AN NP.

Language:

Paper dominated by major and repeated errors (disruptive and nondisruptive).

Many unclear sentences.

Lack of control of sentence structure and verbs.

Noticeably limited vocabulary.

SAMPLE GRADING STANDARDS II

University of California, Davis
English for Nonnative Speakers Undergraduate Program

Final Exam Grading Standards

English 21 — 4-Paragraph Expository Essay Based on Personal Experience

P   Pass   (competent paper)

Organization:

A clearly stated thesis responding to the question.

Topic sentences in each paragraph which are related to the thesis.

An introduction leading to the thesis, and a conclusion.

Appropriate transitions and other coherence devices.

Development:

Unified, coherent paragraphs focused on the question.

Specific, appropriate support and some rudimentary analysis.

May include minor lapses in development.

Language:

Errors do not impede overall understanding.

Developing control of sentence structure and boundaries, with some attempt at sentence variety.

Developing control of verbs: formation, agreement, tenses.

Vocabulary: some attempt to vary word choice and some control of word formation.

P–   Marginal Pass   (adequate paper)

Organization:

A thesis responding to the question.

An attempt at topic sentences.

Introduction and perhaps minimal conclusion.

Some appropriate transitions and other coherence devices.

Development

Generally unified and coherent paragraphs focused on the question.

Specific support.

Language:

An accumulation of errors which sometimes impede understanding.

Emerging control of sentence structure and boundaries and some attempt at sentence variety.

Emerging control of verbs: formation, agreement, tenses.

Vocabulary: some attempt to vary word choice and some control of word formation.

NP+ Marginal Fail (inadequate paper weak in one or more of the following three categories)

Organization:

Unclear or faulty thesis.

Topics of one or more paragraphs unclear or unrelated to thesis.

Transitions missing or generally incorrect.

Development:

Serious coherence problems in one or more paragraphs.

Inadequate support which may veer seriously off topic or noticeably lack specifics.

Analysis lacking.

Language:

Frequent errors which often impede understanding.

Many problems in sentence structure and boundaries; little use of subordination.

Problems with many verbs: formation, agreement, tenses.

Much inaccuracy in word choice and word formation.

NP Clear Fail (very weak paper showing that the writer should not proceed to the next level)

NOTE: NORMALLY THE NP GRADE REFLECTS DEFICIENCIES IN LANGUAGE, NOT IN ORGANIZATION AND/OR DEVELOPMENT. IN RARE CASES, HOWEVER, A PAPER WITH SEVERE ORGANIZATION OR DEVELOPMENT PROBLEMS CAN RECEIVE AN NP.

Language:

Paper dominated by major and repeated errors (disruptive and nondisruptive).

Many unclear sentences.

Lack of control of sentence structure and verbs.

Noticeably limited vocabulary.

SAMPLE GRADING STANDARDS III

University of California

Subject A Scoring Guide

In holistic reading, raters assign each essay to a scoring category according to its dominant characteristics. The categories below describe the characteristics typical of papers at six different levels of competence. All the descriptions take into account that the papers they categorize represent two hours of reading and writing, not a more extended period of drafting and revision.

6 A 6 paper commands attention because of its insightful development and mature style. It presents a cogent response to the text, elaborating that response with well-chosen examples and persuasive reasoning. The 6 paper shows that its writer can usually choose words aptly, use sophisticated sentences effectively, and observe the conventions of written English.

5 A 5 paper is clearly competent. It presents a thoughtful response to the text, elaborating that response with appropriate examples and sensible reasoning. A 5 paper typically has a less fluent and complex style than a 6, but does show that its writer can usually choose words accurately, vary sentences effectively, and observe the conventions of written English.

4 A 4 paper is satisfactory, sometimes marginally so. It presents an adequate response to the text, elaborating that response with sufficient examples and acceptable reasoning. Just as these examples and this reasoning will ordinarily be less developed than those in 5 papers, so will the 4 paper's style be less effective. Nevertheless, a 4 paper shows that its writer can usually choose words of sufficient precision, control sentences of reasonable variety, and observe the conventions of written English.

3 A 3 paper is unsatisfactory in one or more of the following ways. It may respond to the text illogically; it may lack coherent structure or elaboration with examples; it may reflect an incomplete understanding of the text or the topic. Its prose is usually characterized by at least one of the following: frequently imprecise word choice; little sentence variety; occasional major errors in grammar and usage, or frequent minor errors.

2 A 2 paper shows serious weaknesses, ordinarily of several kinds. It frequently presents a simplistic, inappropriate, or incoherent response to the text, one that may suggest some significant misunderstanding of the text or the topic. Its prose is usually characterized by at least one of the following: simplistic or inaccurate word choice; monotonous or fragmented sentence structure; many repeated errors in grammar and usage.

I A 1 paper suggests severe difficulties in reading and writing conventional English. It may disregard the topic's demands, or it may lack any appropriate pattern of structure or development. It may be inappropriately brief. It often has a pervasive pattern of errors in word choice, sentence structure, grammar, and usage.

This scoring guide is used by permission and appears in *An Information Booklet for the Universitywide Subject A Examination* written by George Gadda, UCLA Writing Programs and Subject A Examination Committee Chair. University of California, April 1992, page 3.

BIBLIOGRAPHY

Works Cited

Beavens, M. H. 1977. Individualized goal setting, self-evaluation, and peer evaluation. In *Evaluating writing: Describing, measuring, judging,* eds. C.R. Cooper and L. Odell. Urbana, Ill.: NCTE.

Beebe, L. 1988. *Issues in second language acquisition.* New York: Newbury House.

Brannon, L., and C. H. Knoblauch. 1982. On students' rights to their own texts: A model of teacher response. *College Composition and Communication,* 33:157–166.

Burt, M. K. 1975. Error analysis in the adult EFL classroom. *TESOL Quarterly,* 9(1):53–63.

Burt, M. K., and C. Kiparsky. 1972. *The gooficon: A repair manual for English.* Rowley, Mass.: Newbury House.

Cardelle, M., and L. Corno. 1981. Effects on second language learning of variations in written feedback on homework assignments. *TESOL Quarterly,* 15(3):251–261.

Celce-Murcia, M. 1988. Integrating grammar into the ESL composition class. *Intensive English Programs TESOL Interest Section Newsletter,* 6(1):1–3.

————. 1991. Grammar pedagogy in second and foreign language teaching. *TESOL Quarterly,* 25(3):459–480.

Cohen, A. D. 1987. Student processing of feedback on their compositions. In *Learner strategies in language learning,* eds. A. Wenden and J. Rubin. Englewood Cliffs, N.J.: Prentice-Hall.

Cohen, A. D., and M. Cavalcanti. 1990. Feedback on compositions: Teacher and student verbal reports. In *Second language writing: Research insights for the classroom,* ed. B. Kroll. New York: Cambridge University Press.

Cohen, A. D., and M. Robbins. 1976. Toward assessing interlanguage performance: The relationship between selected errors, learners' characteristics, and learners' explanations. *Language Learning,* 26:45–66.

Connor, U. 1987. Research frontiers in writing analysis. *TESOL Quarterly,* 21(4):677–695.

Connor, U., and R. Kaplan, eds. 1987. *Writing across language: Analysis of L2 text.* Reading, Mass.: Addison-Wesley Publishing Company.

Corder, S. P. 1967. The significance of learner's errors. *International Review of Applied Linguistics,* 5:161–170.

————. 1981. *Error analysis and interlanguage.* Oxford: Oxford University Press.

Cowan, G. 1977. The rhetorician's personae. *College Composition and Communication,* 28:259–262.

Dulay, H. C., and M. K. Burt. 1977. Remarks on creativity in language acquisition. In *Viewpoints on English as a second language,* eds. M. K. Burt, H. Dulay, and M. Finocchiaro. New York: Regents.

Eskey, D. E. 1983. Meanwhile, back in the real world...: Accuracy and fluency in second language teaching. *TESOL Quarterly,* 17(2):315–323.

Fathman, A. K., and E. Whalley. 1985. Teacher treatment of error and student accuracy. Paper presented at the 19th Annual TESOL Convention, New York.

————. 1990. Teacher response to student writing: Focus on form versus content. In *Second language writing: Research insights for the classroom,* ed. B. Kroll. New York: Cambridge University Press.

Flower, L. 1979. Writer-based prose: A cognitive basis for problems in writing. *College English,* 41:19–37.

Friedman, T. 1983. Teaching error, nurturing confusion: Grammar texts, tests, and teachers in the developmental English class. *College English,* 45:390–399.

Gadda, G. 1992. *An information booklet for the universitywide Subject A Examination.* University of California.

Gregg, J. 1986. Contrastive rhetoric: An exploration of Chinese and American expository patterns. *Temple University Working Papers in Composition,* 1–18.

Hairston, M. 1982. The winds of change: Thomas Kuhn and the revolution in the teaching of writing. *College Composition and Communication,* 33:178–190.

Hendrickson, J. M. 1979. Evaluating spontaneous communication through systematic error analysis. *Foreign Language Annals,* 12:357–364.

————. 1980a. Error correction in foreign language teaching: Recent theory, research, and practice. In *Readings on English as a second language,* ed. K. Croft. Cambridge, Mass.: Winthrop.

————. 1980b. The treatment of error in written work. *Modern Language Journal*, 64:216–221.

Hillocks, G., Jr. 1986. *Research on written composition: New directions for teaching.* Urbana, Ill: ERIC Clearinghouse on Reading and Communication Skills and the National Conference on Research in English.

Horning, A. S. 1987. *Teaching writing as a second language.* Carbondale, Ill.: Southern Illinois Press.

Horvath, B. K. 1984. The components of written response: A practical synthesis of current views. *Rhetoric Review*, 2:136–156.

Jones, C. S. 1985. Problems with monitor use in second language composing. In *When a writer can't write,* ed. M. Rose. New York: Guilford Press.

Koreo, K. 1988. Language habits of the Japanese. *English Today,* IV(3):19–25.

Krapels, A. 1990. An overview of second language writing process research. In *Second language writing: Research insights for the classroom,* ed. B. Kroll. New York: Cambridge University Press.

Krashen, S. 1977. The monitor model for adult second language performance. In *Viewpoints on English as a second language,* eds. M. K. Burt, H. Dulay, and M. Finocchiaro. New York: Regents.

————. 1981. *Second language acquisition and second language learning.* Language Methodology Series. Oxford: Pergamon Press.

————. 1982. *Principles and practice in second language acquisition.* New York: Pergamon.

Kroll, B., and J. Schafer. 1978. Error analysis and the teaching of composition. *College Composition and Communication,* 29:243–248.

Lalande, J. F. 1982. Reducing composition errors: An experiment. *Modern Language Journal,* 66:140–149.

Larsen-Freeman, D. 1991. Second language acquisition: Staking out the territory. *TESOL Quarterly,* 25(2):315–350.

Lees, E. 1979. Evaluating student writing. *College Composition and Communication,* 30:370–374.

Leki, I. 1986. ESL student preferences in written error correction. Paper presented at the Southeast Regional TESOL Conference, Atlanta, Ga.

————. 1990. Coaching from the margins. In *Second language writing: Research insights for the classroom,* ed. B. Kroll. New York: Cambridge University Press.

Mallonee, B. C., and J. R. Breihan. 1985. Responding to students' drafts: Interdisciplinary consensus. *College Composition and Communication,* 36:213–231.

Meyers, M. 1985. *The teacher–researcher: How to study writing in the classroom.* Urbana, Ill.: ERIC Clearinghouse on Reading and Communication Skills and the National Council of Teachers of English.

Murray, D. 1982. Teach writing as a process not product. In *Learning by teaching: Selected articles on writing and teaching.* Portsmouth, N.H.: Boynton, Cook.

Radecki, P. M., and J. M. Swales. 1988. ESL student reaction to written comments on their written work. *System,* 16(3):355–365.

Raimes, A. 1983. Tradition and resolution in ESL teaching. *TESOL Quarterly,* 17(4):535–552.

————. 1985. What unskilled ESL students do as they write: A classroom study of composing. *TESOL Quarterly,* 19(2):229–258.

————. 1986. Teaching ESL writing: Fitting what we do to what we know. *The Writing Instructor,* Summer:153–190.

————. 1991. Errors: Windows into the mind. *College ESL,* 1(2):55–64.

Reid, J. 1988. *The process of writing.* Englewood Cliffs, N.J.: Prentice-Hall.

————. 1992. Helping students write for an academic audience. In *The multicultural classroom: Readings for content-area teachers,* eds. P. Richard-Amato and M. Snow. White Plains, N.Y.: Longman.

Rizzo, B. 1982. Systems analysis for correcting English compositions. *College Composition and Communication,* 33:320–322.

Robb, T., S. Ross, and I. Shortreed. 1986. Salience of feedback on error and its effect on EFL writing quality. *TESOL Quarterly,* 20(1):83–95.

Santos, T. 1988. Professors' reactions to the academic writing of nonnative-speaking students. *TESOL Quarterly,* 22(1):69–90.

Selinker, L. 1974. Interlanguage. Reprinted in *Error analysis: Perspectives on second language acquisition,* ed. J.C. Richards. London: Longman.

Semke, H. D. 1984. The effects of the red pen. *Foreign Language Annals*, 17:195–202.

Silva, T. 1989. A critical review of ESL composing process research. Paper presented at the 23rd Annual TESOL Convention, San Antonio, Tex. ERIC Document Reproduction Service No. ED 305820.

Sommers, N. 1982. Responding to student writing. *College Composition and Communication*, 33:148–156.

Sridhar, S. N. 1980. Contrastive analysis, error analysis, and interlanguage. In *Readings on English as a second language*, ed. K. Croft. Cambridge, Mass.: Winthrop.

Vann, R. J., D. E. Meyer, and F. O. Lorenz. 1984. Error gravity: A study of faculty opinion of ESL errors. *TESOL Quarterly*, 18(3):427–440.

Vigil, N. A., and J. W. Oller. 1976. Rule fossilization: A tentative model. *Language Learning*, 26:281–295.

Vygotsky, L. S. 1978. *Mind and society: The development of higher psychological processes*. Ed. M. Cole et al. Cambridge, Mass.: Harvard University Press.

Walz, J. C. 1982. Error correction techniques for the foreign language classroom. Language in Education, Theory and Practice, No. 50. ERIC Document Reproduction Service No. ED 217704 FLO 12967.

Williams, J. 1981. The phenomenology of error. *College Composition and Communication*, 32:152–168.

Witbeck, M. C. 1976. Peer correction procedures for intermediate and advanced ESL composition lessons. *TESOL Quarterly*, 10(3):321–326.

Xu, G. Q. 1989. Helping ESL students improve unEnglish sentences in one-to-one conferences. ERIC Document Reproduction Service No. ED 304003 FLO 17798.

Zamel, V. 1982. Writing: The process of discovering meaning. *TESOL Quarterly*, 16(2):195–209.

————. 1983. The composing process of advanced ESL students: Six case studies. *TESOL Quarterly*, 17(2):165–187.

————. 1985. Responding to student writing. *TESOL Quarterly*, 19(1):79–101.

————. 1987. Recent research on writing pedagogy. *TESOL Quarterly*, 21(4):697–715.

Categorized Bibliography

A. Composition for Native Speakers

Native-Speaker Composition—State of the Art

Flower, L. 1979. Writer-based prose: A cognitive basis for problems in writing. *College English,* 41:19–37.

Hairston, M. 1982. The winds of change: Thomas Kuhn and the revolution in the teaching of writing. *College Composition and Communication,* 33:178–190.

Murray, D. 1982. Teach writing as a process not product. In *Learning by teaching: Selected articles on writing and teaching.* Portsmouth, N.H.: Boynton, Cook.

Schroeder, T. S. 1973. The effects of positive and corrective written teacher feedback on selected writing behaviors of fourth-grade children. Unpublished doctoral dissertation, University of Kansas.

Response to Student Writing

Beavens, M. H. 1977. Individualized goal setting, self-evaluation, and peer evaluation. In *Evaluating writing: Describing, measuring, judging,* eds. C.R. Cooper and L. Odell. Urbana, Ill.: NCTE.

Brannon, L., and C. H. Knoblauch. 1982. On students' rights to their own texts: A model of teacher response. *College Composition and Communication,* 33:157–166.

Cowan, G. 1977. The rhetorician's personae. *College Composition and Communication,* 28:259–262.

Hillocks, G., Jr. 1982. The interaction of instruction, teacher comment, and revision in teaching the composing process. *Research in the Teaching of English,* 16(3):261–278.

————. 1986. *Research on written composition: New directions for teaching.* Urbana, Ill: ERIC Clearinghouse on Reading and Communication Skills and the National Conference on Research in English.

Horvath, B. K. 1984. The components of written response: A practical synthesis of current views. *Rhetoric Review,* 2:136–156.

Lees, E. 1979. Evaluating student writing. *College Composition and Communication,* 30:370–374.

Mallonee, B. C., and J. R. Breihan. 1985. Responding to students' drafts: Interdisciplinary consensus. *College Composition and Communication,* 36:213–231.

Sommers, N. 1982. Responding to student writing. *College Composition and Communication,* 33:148–156.

Vygotsky, L. S. 1978. *Mind and society: The development of higher psychological processes.* Ed. M. Cole et al. Cambridge, Mass.: Harvard University Press.

Theory on Sentence-Level Error

Bartholomae, D. 1980. The study of error. *College Composition and Communication,* 31:253–269.

Connors, R. J. 1985. Mechanical correctness as a focus in composition instruction. *College Composition and Communication,* 36:61–72.

Friedman, T. 1983. Teaching error, nurturing confusion: Grammar texts, tests, and teachers in the developmental English class. *College English,* 45:390–399.

Shaughnessy, M. 1977. *Error and expectation.* New York: Oxford University Press.

Rizzo, B. 1982. Systems analysis for correcting English compositions. *College Composition and Communication,* 33:320–322.

Williams, J. 1981. The phenomenology of error. *College Composition and Communication,* 32:152–168.

B. ESL Composition

ESL Teaching—State of the Art

Celce-Murcia, M. 1988. Integrating grammar into the ESL composition class. *Intensive English Programs TESOL Interest Section Newsletter,* 6(1):1–3.

————. 1991. Grammar pedagogy in second and foreign language teaching. *TESOL Quarterly,* 25(3):459–480.

Celce-Murcia, M., and S. Hilles. 1988. *Techniques and resources in teaching grammar.* New York: Oxford University Press.

Connor, U. 1987. Research frontiers in writing analysis. *TESOL Quarterly*, 21(4):677–695.

Eskey, D. E. 1983. Meanwhile, back in the real world…: Accuracy and fluency in second language teaching. *TESOL Quarterly*, 17(2):315–323.

Frodesen, J. 1991. Grammar in writing. In *Teaching English as a second or foreign language*, ed. M. Celce-Murcia. Boston: Newbury House.

Raimes, A. 1983. Tradition and resolution in ESL teaching. *TESOL Quarterly*, 17(4):535–552.

———. 1986. Teaching ESL writing: Fitting what we do to what we know. *The Writing Instructor*, Summer:153–190.

Reid, J. 1988. *The process of writing*. Englewood Cliffs, N.J.: Prentice-Hall.

———. 1992. Helping students write for an academic audience. In *The multicultural classroom: Readings for content-area teachers*, eds. P. Richard-Amato and M. Snow. White Plains, N.Y.: Longman.

Zamel, V. 1982. Writing: The process of discovering meaning. *TESOL Quarterly*, 16(2):195–209.

———. 1987. Recent research on writing pedagogy. *TESOL Quarterly*, 21(4):697–715.

Responding to the ESL Paper

Fathman, A. K., and E. Whalley. 1990. Teacher response to student writing: Focus on form versus content. In *Second language writing: Research insights for the classroom*, ed. B. Kroll. New York: Cambridge University Press.

Leki, I. 1990. Coaching from the margins. In *Second language writing: Research insights for the classroom*, ed. B. Kroll. New York: Cambridge University Press.

Witbeck, M. C. 1976. Peer correction procedures for intermediate and advanced ESL composition lessons. *TESOL Quarterly*, 10(3):321–326.

Zamel, V. 1985. Responding to student writing. *TESOL Quarterly*, 19(1):79–101.

ESL Student Processing of Feedback on Papers

Cardelle, M., and L. Corno. 1981. Effects on second language learning of variations in written feedback on homework assignments. *TESOL Quarterly*, 15(3):251–261.

Cohen, A. D. 1987. Student processing of feedback on their compositions. In *Learner strategies in language learning,* eds. A. Wenden and J. Rubin. Englewood Cliffs, N.J.: Prentice-Hall.

Cohen, A. D., and M. Cavalcanti. 1990. Feedback on compositions: Teacher and student verbal reports. In *Second language writing: Research insights for the classroom,* ed. B. Kroll. New York: Cambridge University Press.

Lalande, J. F. 1982. Reducing composition errors: An experiment. *Modern Language Journal,* 66:140–149.

Leki, I. 1986. ESL student preferences in written error correction. Paper presented at the Southeast Regional TESOL Conference, Atlanta, Ga.

————. 1991. The preferences of ESL students for error correction in college-level writing classes. *Foreign Language Annals,* 24:203–18.

Radecki, P. M., and J. M. Swales. 1988. ESL student reaction to written comments on their written work. *System,* 16(3):355–365.

Robb, T., S. Ross, and I. Shortreed. 1986. Salience of feedback on error and its effect on EFL writing quality. *TESOL Quarterly,* 20(1):83–95.

Semke, H. D. 1984. The effects of the red pen. *Foreign Language Annals,* 17:195–202.

Language Acquisition

Beebe, L. 1988. *Issues in second language acquisition.* New York: Newbury House.

Krashen, S. 1981. *Second language acquisition and second language learning.'* Language Methodology Series. Oxford: Pergamon Press.

————. 1982. *Principles and practice in second language acquisition.* New York: Pergamon.

Larsen-Freeman, D. 1991. Second language acquisition: Staking out the territory. *TESOL Quarterly,* 25(2):315–350.

Larsen-Freeman, D., and M. Long. 1991. *An introduction to second language acquisition research.* London and New York: Longman.

Error Analysis

Burt, M. K. 1975. Error analysis in the adult EFL classroom. *TESOL Quarterly,* 9(1):53–63.

Burt, M. K., and C. Kiparsky. 1972. *The gooficon: A repair manual for English.* Rowley, Mass.: Newbury House.

Corder, S. P. 1967. The significance of learners' errors. *International Review of Applied Linguistics,* 5:161–170.

————. 1981. *Error analysis and interlanguage.* Oxford: Oxford University Press.

Dulay, H. C., and M. K. Burt. 1977. Remarks on creativity in language acquisition. In *Viewpoints on English as a second language,* eds. M. K. Burt, H. Dulay, and M. Finocchiaro. New York: Regents.

Hendrickson, J. M. 1979. Evaluating spontaneous communication through systematic error analysis. *Foreign Language Annals,* 12:357–364.

————. 1980a. Error correction in foreign language teaching: Recent theory, research, and practice. In *Readings on English as a second language,* ed. K. Croft. Cambridge, Mass.: Winthrop.

————. 1980b. The treatment of error in written work. *Modern Language Journal,* 64:216–221.

Kroll, B., and J. Schafer. 1978. Error analysis and the teaching of composition. *College Composition and Communication,* 29:243–248.

Raimes, A. 1991. Errors: Windows into the mind. *College ESL,* 1(2):55–64.

Sridhar, S. N. 1980. Contrastive analysis, error analysis, and interlanguage. In *Readings on English as a second language,* ed. K. Croft. Cambridge, Mass.: Winthrop.

Walz, J. C. 1982. Error correction techniques for the foreign language classroom. Language in Education, Theory and Practice, No. 50. ERIC Document Reproduction Service No. ED 217704 FLO 12967.

Xu, G. Q. 1989. Helping ESL students improve unEnglish sentences in one-to-one conferences. ERIC Document Reproduction Service No. ED 304003 FLO 17798.

Interlanguage and Fossilization

Cohen, A. D., and M. Robbins. 1976. Toward assessing interlanguage performance: The relationship between selected errors, learners' characteristics, and learners' explanations. *Language Learning,* 26:45–66.

Corder, S. P. 1967. The significance of learners' errors. *International Review of Applied Linguistics,* 5:161–170.

————. 1981. *Error analysis and interlanguage.* Oxford: Oxford University Press.

Horning, A. S. 1987. *Teaching writing as a second language.* Carbondale, Ill.: Southern Illinois Press.

Selinker, L. 1974. Interlanguage. Reprinted in *Error analysis: Perspectives on second language acquisition,* ed. J.C. Richards. London: Longman.

Vigil, N. A., and J. W. Oller. 1976. Rule fossilization: A tentative model. *Language Learning,* 26:281–295.

Monitor Theory

Jones, C. S. 1985. Problems with monitor use in second language composing. In *When a writer can't write,* ed. M. Rose. New York: Guilford Press.

Krashen, S. 1977. The monitor model for adult second language performance. In *Viewpoints on English as a second language,* eds. M. K. Burt, H. Dulay, and M. Finocchiaro. New York: Regents.

————. 1981. *Second language acquisition and second language learning.* Language Methodology Series. Oxford: Pergamon Press.

ESL Writing Process

Krapels, A. 1990. An overview of second language writing process research. In *Second language writing: Research insights for the classroom,* ed. B. Kroll. New York: Cambridge University Press.

Raimes, A. 1985. What unskilled ESL students do as they write: A classroom study of composing. *TESOL Quarterly,* 19(2):229–258.

Silva, T. 1989. A critical review of ESL composing process research. Paper presented at the 23rd Annual TESOL Convention, San Antonio, Tex. ERIC Document Reproduction Service No. ED 305820.

Zamel, V. 1983. The composing process of advanced ESL students: Six case studies. *TESOL Quarterly,* 17(2):165–187.

Faculty Response to ESL Errors

Kresovich, B. W. 1988. Error gravity: Perceptions of native-speaking and non-native-speaking faculty in EFL. ERIC Document Reproduction Service No. ED 311732.

McGirt, J. D. 1984. The effect of morphological and syntactic errors on the holistic scores of native and non-native compositions. Unpublished M.A. thesis in TESL, University of California, Los Angeles.

Santos, T. 1988. Professors' reactions to the academic writing of nonnative-speaking students. *TESOL Quarterly,* 22(1):69–90.

Vann, R. J., D. E. Meyer, and F. O. Lorenz. 1984. Error gravity: A study of faculty opinion of ESL errors. *TESOL Quarterly,* 18(3):427–440.

Contrastive Rhetoric

Beebe, L. 1988. *Issues in second language acquisition.* New York: Newbury House.

Connor, U., and R. Kaplan, eds. 1987. *Writing across language: Analysis of L2 text.* Reading, Mass.: Addison-Wesley Publishing Company.

Gregg, J. 1986. Contrastive rhetoric: An exploration of Chinese and American expository patterns. *Temple University Working Papers in Composition,* 1–18.

Koreo, K. 1988. Language habits of the Japanese. *English Today,* IV(3):19–25.

Meyers, M. 1985. *The teacher–researcher: How to study writing in the classroom.* Urbana, Ill.: ERIC Clearinghouse on Reading and Communication Skills and the National Council of Teachers of English.

ANSWER KEY

to Exercises in

Writing Clearly:

An Editing Guide

■ Answer Key: Unit 1

EXERCISE I

<u>I</u> 1. I **have been** interested in physics since high school.

<u>I</u> 2. Having computer skills is essential for a college freshman, and I **have decided** to learn how to use a computer.

<u>I</u> 3. Roger **is majoring** in environmental engineering on this campus.

<u>I</u> 4. Since she was a child, she **has liked** sports, especially water sports, such as swimming and water skiing.

<u>C</u> 5.

<u>I</u> 6. Mario **graduated** as a veterinarian in January 1989.

<u>C</u> 7.

<u>I</u> 8. Human beings make mistakes. Sometimes we **do** things we **greatly regret**.

<u>C</u> 9.

<u>I</u> 10. The professor **gave** an introduction to the course yesterday, the first day of class.

<u>I</u> 11. There are rumors that tuition **will be** higher next year.

<u>C</u> 12.

<u>C</u> 13.

<u>I</u> 14. My Ph.D. research **is taking** a great deal longer than I expected.

<u>I</u> 15. In my opinion, voting in elections is very important.

EXERCISE 2

helps (help)
is (be)
have learned (learn)
plans (plan)
goes (go)
writes (write)
has (have)
will spend (OR **is going to spend**) (spend)
schedules (schedule)
sets (set)
is (is)
disciplines (discipline)
has completed (complete)
invited (invite)
refused (refuse)
had not finished (not finish)
know (know that)
will make (OR **am going to make**) (make)

EXERCISE 3 (Two options are possible.)

Option A

I have a positive attitude toward writing in English. When I first came to America, I was very confused about using English, a new and strange language. But as time **went** by, my feeling toward the language **began** to change. I **forced** myself to write even though it was hard at first. I **wrote** a lot, and I **became** more confident each time I **wrote**. Now, although I am more confident about writing, I still have many problems to overcome. I find that writing takes a great deal of time and one has to be patient and disciplined in order to be good at it. At times, I **am** frustrated and impatient with my writing. In fact, sometimes I sit for hours and cannot write even a word. Nevertheless, despite my frustration and long hours of work, I tend to have a positive attitude toward writing in English. Even though English is not my native language, I have found that I simply like to write.

Option B

I have a positive attitude toward writing in English. When I first came to America, I was very confused about using English, a new and strange language. But as time **has gone** by, my feeling toward the language **has begun** to change. I **have forced** myself to write even though it was hard at first. I **have written** a lot, and I **have become** (OR **am becoming**) more confident each time I write. Now, although I am more confident about writing, I still have many problems to overcome. I find that writing takes a great deal of time and one has to be patient and disciplined in order to be good at it. At times, I **am** frustrated and impatient with my writing. In fact, sometimes I sit for hours and cannot write even a word. Nevertheless, despite my frustration and long hours of work, I tend to have a positive attitude toward writing in English. Even though English is not my native language, I have found that I simply like to write.

EXERCISE 4

Children of immigrants who do not speak English often **function** more like adults than children. As a child of immigrant parents myself, I have often had to act as an adult. Ever since my family arrived here five years ago, I **have taken** care of them in many ways. I have had to pay the rent, the utilities, the telephone, and any other payments. I **have translated** (OR **translate**) letters from English to Italian for the whole family. When a family member **has been** (OR **is**) sick, I **have gone** (OR **go**) along to the doctor to explain the problem and to translate the doctor's suggestions. I believe it has been good for me to do all these things because **it has prepared** me for what I **will face** when I am living on my own. Having adult responsibilities **has given** (OR **gives**) me the chance to understand what the world is like outside of my home. It **has provided** (OR **provides**) me with hands-on training and is beneficial for me.

EXERCISE 5

Luckily for me, at the very end of my first semester here at college, my grades changed for the better. My Chemistry 1A class last semester is one example. At the start of the semester, I did not understand the materials or the problems. I was confused when I read and **tried** to solve problems. Even though I **did** the homework and **went** to all the laboratory sessions, my understanding did not seem to improve. In fact, on my first and second midterms, I **received** a D and an F. After receiving those two grades, I **started** to realize that I had to change the way I was studying. I **decided** to put myself on a strict schedule and to go to the library every day after dinner. I **continued** to follow this plan until **the end** of the semester. Even now, I still cannot believe how well I **did** on my final. I received a B on the final and a C for the semester. This is what I think **happened:** When I reviewed all the materials systematically, I **was** able to understand principles of chemistry that I **had** not **understood** before.

EXERCISE 6

Answers will vary.

■ Answer Key: Unit 2

EXERCISE I

   I   1. I have **lived** in the United States for two years.

   C   2.

   I   3. By **exercising** on a regular basis, an athlete can build a strong body, maintain muscle flexibility, and develop stamina.

   I   4. In the case of my younger sister, punishment seems to be an effective way to make her **behave** better.

   I   5. If I can succeed in college and **go** to medical school, I will have the opportunity to pursue the career I want and possibly even become famous.

   I   6. My instructor **is** not **pleased** with my lack of participation in class.

   C   7. I believe that I have a good chance of **getting** into medical school.

   I   8. Scientists are currently **trying** to find a cure for AIDS.

   C   9.

   I 10. I did not **expect** you to call me so soon.

   I 11. I have been wearing my favorite jeans so much that they are becoming rather worn **out.**

   I 12. By the time I got home, my roommate had already **cooked,** even though it was my turn to make dinner.

   C 13.

   I 14. My best friend asked me to take a vacation and to **come** to California for a visit.

EXERCISE 2   Sample Answers:

1. I avoided **talking** to my friend last night because I am angry at him.
2. Many students prefer **studying** late at night rather than during the day.
3. By **communicating,** we can work out our problems.
4. These boxes are too heavy for me. Could you help me **carry** them?
5. The coach encouraged the team to **practice** regularly.
6. One of my goals is **to go** to medical school.

7. Many students dislike **taking exams**.
8. **Gardening** is one of my hobbies.
9. I am good at **using the computer**.
10. A classmate let me **borrow** his notes when I was not able to **come** to class last week.
11. It is easy **to go** there by train.

EXERCISE 3

1. My neighbors make so much noise that I have trouble concentrating **on** my work.
2. I dreamed **about** (OR **of**) you last night.
3. I don't know if I can ever forgive you **for** lying to me.
4. Are you interested **in** going camping with us next weekend?
5. My advisor insisted **on** my submitting a research proposal by January.
6. I will have to think **about** what you have said before I give you an answer.
7. I am hopeful that I will succeed **in** finishing my B.S. by next year.
8. My parents don't object **to** my borrowing their car on weekends.
9. We want to take advantage **of** the nice weather and go on a picnic.

EXERCISE 4

to walk/walking (walk)
to relax (relax)
enjoy/to enjoy (enjoy)
stroll/am strolling (stroll)
relax/to relax (relax)
walking (walk)
to continue (continue)

EXERCISE 5

It takes a great deal of courage for a person to leave his or her family and **start** life all over again in another country. The person not only must face many changes alone must also separate from friends and rely on letters as a means of **sharing** thoughts. The new environment and the new setting make even the bravest individual **feel** scared, as he or she encounters many sudden changes and **undergoes** many kinds of struggles in a short period of time. Despite these difficulties, **going** abroad as an immigrant has many benefits. **Going** abroad gives a person the chance to see the world, to face new challenges, to make new friends, and **to gain** more knowledge about people and places. Before I came to the United States, I had many expectations. I thought that life in this country would be similar to life in my country. However, after being here for five months, I have **come** to the conclusion that life in the United States is entirely different from what I had **expected**.

EXERCISE 6

Answers will vary.

■ Answer Key: Unit 3

EXERCISE I

1. Past: Bob might have been joking about his decision to quit school.
2. Past: Lian could have been joking about her poor handwriting skills.
3. Past: When he was on the track team, Max could run a mile in 4 minutes, 30 seconds.
4. Past: Jill must have been tired after working all day yesterday.
5. Past: Because Lydia needed to get a good grade on her chemistry midterm, she had to study last night.
6. Past: I should have exercised more often last year.
7. Past: You ought to have sent your roommate's parents a thank you note since you spent the weekend at their house.
8. Past: My supervisor must have been sick since she did not attend the office barbecue over the weekend.
9. Past: Mary may not have had time to call her parents last night.
10. Past: My roommate had to do the shopping last week.

EXERCISE 2

1. She must have left early.
2. It might rain./It may rain.
3. She had to go to Sacramento.
4. She should send a thank-you note.
5. She may/might allow us to leave early.
6. The house must have cost a lot of money.
7. I should have asked him to help.
8. When I was young, I could speak French, but I have forgotten it.
9. My housemate could have washed the dishes last night, but she went out instead.
10. We could camp out on our way to the Grand Canyon.

EXERCISE 3

  I   1. My brother must **have** forgotten to call me.

  I   2. My brother could have **called** me while I was at the library.

  I   3. My brother may **call** late tonight.

  I   4. I did not have time to stop at the store because I **had to stay** (OR **stayed**) late at the office to finish my work.

  C   5.

  I   6. I got a speeding ticket! I should not have **been** driving over the speed limit on the freeway.

  C   7.

  C   8.

EXERCISE 4

Grand Canyon National Park in Arizona is a paradise for nature

                                    1   *(1) shows future time*

lovers and outdoor enthusiasts. Visitors <u>will be</u> awed by the fabulous

view of the canyon, its vast depth and beautifully colored walls. The

National Park Headquarters and Visitor Center is at the South Rim,

                               2   *(2) suggests an option*

where visitors <u>can pick up</u> information about the park there. Visitors

                               3   *(3) suggests an option*

who have only a little time to spend <u>can view</u> the canyon from either

                                       4   *(4) shows possibility*

the North Rim or the South Rim. People who have more time <u>may</u>

<u>want</u> to see more of the Grand Canyon than just the North or South

                               5   *(5) suggests an option*

Rim. Visitors <u>can drive</u> along parts of the rim or hike down into the

                               6   *(6) suggests an option*

canyon on various trails. In fact, hikers <u>can walk</u> or <u>ride</u> a mule all

the way to the bottom of the canyon to the Colorado River. How-

                               7   *(7) indicates a necessity*

ever, hikers <u>must be sure</u> to drink plenty of water to avoid dehydra-

                               8   *(8) suggests a possibility*

tion as the weather <u>can be</u> extremely hot and dry. At the bottom,

          9   *(9) suggests an option*

hikers <u>can stay</u> at either Phantom Ranch, which consists of cabins

and dormitories, or at an adjacent campground. Perhaps the best

way to see the canyon, however, is to float down the Colorado River

either on a rubber raft or in a wooden dory. Seeing the canyon from

this perspective is spectacular, but people who are afraid of big

                               10   *(10) gives advice*

whitewater <u>should not take</u> this trip since some of the Colorado

River rapids are among the biggest in the world. For most visitors, a

                               11   *(11) shows an expectation*

trip to the Grand Canyon <u>should be</u> a truly unforgettable experience.

EXERCISE 5

should have waited (wait/advisability)
could have started (start/opportunity)
should have proofread (proofread/advisability)
could have added (add/opportunity)
had to stay up (stay up/necessity)

EXERCISE 6

Answers will vary.

■ Answer Key: Unit 4

EXERCISE I

__I__ 1. If I **had** a car, I would not ask friends to take me shopping.

__I__ 2. If Margaret had slept more, she would not **have** had trouble staying awake during the chemistry lecture yesterday.

__C__ 3.

__I__ 4. If I **go** to Los Angeles next week, I will see all my friends.

__I__ 5. If Peter **went** to the bookstore later today, he **could** buy two tapes for the price of one. (OR **goes, can**)

__I__ 6. If Edith had not had to turn in her paper today, she would **have** skipped class.

__I__ 7. If the weather is nice, Marcella always **takes** a walk after dinner.

__I__ 8. If I could **find** a ride home this weekend, I would give my parents a surprise visit.

__C__ 9.

__C__ 10.

EXERCISE 2

1. If the city **had expanded** the parking space downtown, we would not have had to park so far away from the movies.

2. When my roommate **snores** loudly, I cannot sleep.

3. Celebrities often get very depressed if they **do not appear** in the news.

4. If we **had not had** to take an exam on the conditional, we might not have learned it.

5. Maya **will not pass** her driving test unless she calms down.

6. If it **were** winter, all these trees would be covered with snow.

7. Had it not rained, the farmers **would have lost** all their crops.

8. If the airplane had not had a mechanical problem, we **would** probably **have arrived** (OR **would** probably **be arriving**) in Tucson by now.

9. We could have been lying (OR could/would be lying) on the beach in Mexico right now if we had been able to get our visas on time.

10. I would try to find more opportunities to speak English if I were you.

EXERCISE 3   Sample Answers:

1. If Jennifer did not have to be in class right now, she could go to the library.

2. I would have gotten to class earlier if I had gotten up when my alarm went off.

3. If I had gotten enough sleep last night, I would have stayed awake in class (OR I would not be yawning now).

4. I would complain about this class if I were not learning.

5. If Vincent has time later, he will help me with my calculus problems.

6. If I had had time during the weekend, I would have revised my essay.

7. If I had a little extra money, I would buy some new software for my computer.

8. If students are given too much to learn, they cannot absorb all of it.

9. If the tuition were raised, I would have to transfer to a cheaper school.

10. Even if the professor had canceled class on Tuesday, I still would not have profited from the extra time to study.

EXERCISE 4

1. If George and Anita go on their picnic, it might rain.
   If George and Anita went on their picnic, it could rain.

2. If Martin tries to exit now, he might get into an accident.
   If Martin exited now, he could get into an accident.

3. If Mark had not bought the computer last year, he would not have done so well in school.
   If Mark had not put himself into debt, he would not be having so many financial problems now.

4. If Chi Wai moves to the dormitory, he will be able to socialize with his friends.
   If Chi Wai moved to the dormitory, he would not be able to cook, even though he would be with his friends.

EXERCISE 5

Another point students should consider when they choose a major is not whether it will make them rich but whether it will at least ensure them enough income to support themselves and their family. It is true that liberal arts majors often get lower-paying jobs than do science majors; however, if people are interested in the liberal arts, they should study those majors. Even though the jobs they get might not enable them to buy big houses or fancy cars, the jobs would allow them to support themselves easily. For instance, my cousin who majored in English now writes novels and is going to publish his first novel in July. Although he has gone through many hardships as a writer, he still has enough income to support his family. He likes writing very much and wants to write as long as he lives. Even though his parents wanted him to become a doctor, it would have been hard for my cousin if he **had** majored in biology. He would probably

have been very uncomfortable and **have felt** pressured and stressed in his classes. If he then **had gotten** a job he did not like in that field, he might **have earned** a high salary but he might have found himself with an ulcer. If we **look** at my cousin as an example, it becomes clear that students must choose a major that is mentally satisfying, not a major that guarantees a big income.

■ Answer Key: Unit 5

EXERCISE I (Incorrect sentences are rewritten.)

<u> I </u> 1. Molecular genetics is a field that is (OR which is) progressing very fast.

<u> I </u> 2. They should be proud instead of embarrassed to know their native language.

<u> I </u> 3. Whenever I see the colors red and green, I think of Christmas. (OR The colors red and green remind me of Christmas.)

<u> C </u> 4.

<u> I </u> 5. She wonders whether studying so hard is worth it.

<u> I </u> 6. Wong is a Chinese woman who grew up in the U.S. and who finds her native language very difficult.

<u> I </u> 7. Engineering 10 is the course that I spend the least time on. (OR...is the course on which I spend the least time.)

<u> I </u> 8. Room 194 Chemistry is one of the largest classrooms on my campus, and it can hold around 500 students.

OR

Room 194 Chemistry, one of the largest classrooms on my campus, can hold around 500 students.

<u> I </u> 9. There are two reasons why I am scared of writing English.

OR

There are two reasons for my being scared of writing English.

<u> I </u> 10. Going to school and working full time is hard.

OR

To go to school and work full time is hard.

<u> I </u> 11. As they grow up, many children develop attitudes they will later have as adults.

<u> C </u> 12.

<u> C </u> 13.

<u> I </u> 14. The engineering professor assumes that the students have a strong background in mathematics.

<u> I </u> 15. Space-shuttle astronauts need to be prepared for every obstacle that they will encounter.

<u> I </u> 16. It is impossible for a person to live without being influenced by the society around him or her.

<u> I </u> 17. Many high school students are more interested in learning about current events than about events that (OR which) have happened in the past.

___I___ 18. The editor doubts that the article will be of interest to many of the readers of the magazine.

___C___ 19.

___I___ 20. As we can see, Marcella is very lucky to have gotten a full scholarship for four years of college work.

EXERCISE 2

A.1. That Jack arrived late to the meeting and that he was not prepared angered his supervisor.

> OR

Jack's arriving late to the meeting and his not being prepared angered his supervisor.

2. I hope to introduce you to Dr. Wood, my thesis advisor and chair of the Chemistry Department.

3. Correct

4. His summer job involves washing laboratory equipment, setting up new experiments, and recording some basic data.

5. Growing up in a large family and having working parents may have resulted in Elizabeth's not getting much individual attention from her parents.

Sample Answers:

B.1. Three things I enjoy doing on weekends are relaxing by the pool, going on day trips, and visiting friends.

2. Two things I have learned since I have been a student here are that it is essential to keep up with the assigned reading and that it is important to take breaks regularly.

3. In my opinion, a good teacher must be organized, approachable, and committed to teaching.

EXERCISE 3

A.1. that/who

2. whose

3. whom

4. that/which

5. whose/where/in which

B.1. Genetic engineering, a newly-developed technology, is expected to help immensely in agriculture.

> OR

Genetic engineering is a newly-developed technology that is expected to help immensely in agriculture.

2. The man whose house I am renting is a lawyer.

3. The people we were waiting for were late.

   OR

   The people that we were waiting for were late.

   OR

   The people whom we were waiting for were late.

4. She borrowed a bicycle the tires of which were slightly flat.

   OR

   She borrowed a bicycle whose tires were slightly flat.

   OR

   She borrowed a bicycle that had slightly flat tires.

5. Today, Michael plans to do the lab experiment that (OR which) he was unable to do last week.

6. The student that (OR who) was asked to make a speech at commencement got the highest grades in the class.

   OR

   The student that (OR who) got the highest grades in the class was asked to make a speech at commencement.

7. Bike riders who (OR that) do not stop at stop signs may be given either a warning or a ticket.

C.1. The person whom (OR with whom) I went to the movies with fell asleep during the film.

2. A student who plagiarizes on a paper will fail the paper and possibly the whole course for which (OR in which) he wrote the paper.

3. Correct

4. I wrote a thank-you note to the people whose home I visited over the holidays.

5. The instructor who (OR that) teaches that course is very well organized.

EXERCISE 4

*Some couples are childless have made a decision not to have children. *This kind of family rapidly growing in the United States. These couples choose to be childless for various reasons. *However, I personally have a hard time understanding people choose to live without children.

Many couples think that this world is not "good enough" for children to grow up in. *Other couples think that too much time and money to raise children. *Still others want to focus on developing their careers rather than raise children.

*I find it hard to understand these reasons that not having children. *For me, having children one of the most essential parts of life. It would be hard for me to view a career as being more important than having a family of my own. I am sure I would feel disappointed with my life when I got old if I did not have children or grandchildren. *I understand that the world overpopulation, but having children is one of our basic instincts. Although I do not want many children, I certainly hope to have one or two of my own.

Sample revised sentences:

1. Some couples who (OR that) are childless have made a decision not to have children.

2. This kind of family is rapidly growing in the United States.

3. However, I personally have a hard time understanding people who choose to live without children. (OR I personally have a hard time understanding people's choosing to live without children.) (OR However, I personally have a hard time understanding how people live without children.)

4. Other couples think that it takes (OR it requires) too much time and money to raise children (OR that too much time and money are need to raise children).

5. Still others want to focus on developing their careers rather than raising children.

6. Find it hard to understand these reasons for not having children.

7. For me, having children is one of the most essential parts of life.

8. I understand that the world is overpopulated, but having children is one of our basic instincts.

■ Answer Key: Unit 6

EXERCISE 1

1. I do not really know what this issue is all about.
2. I have already been advanced to candidacy for my Ph.D.
3. The only concern I have is how much it will cost the students to pay the rent.
4. Correct.
5. Correct.
6. Tomas is planning to have a surprise birthday party for Luis.
7. I haven't gotten my term paper back even though I handed it in a week ago.
8. I am going to buy my father a beautiful green silk tie for his birthday.
9. Correct
10. The professor comes to class on time everyday.

    OR

    Everyday, the professor comes to class on time.

EXERCISE 2 Sample Answers:

1. The professor said he doesn't know when the midterm will be.
2. Your term paper does not cover how you analyzed your results.
3. I'm sorry but I did not understand what you just said.

EXERCISE 3

Although you can learn vocabulary in your English class and from your textbooks, you may never have considered the many other handy reference tools that you can use to build up your vocabulary. Have you ever thought, for instance, what a great teacher the supermarket can be? If you think about it, everything has either a label or a sign, making it easy for you to connect <u>the words with the product,</u> such as the words *chocolate chips* on the label with a window on the package that lets you see the chips, or a picture of diced tomatoes on a can. Besides, if you <u>are still not sure</u> about <u>what a product is,</u> you can ask <u>another customer in the store</u> to help you, and you will be practicing your spoken English besides. Have you ever thought, too, what a great resource the Yellow Pages of the telephone directory can be? If you look at the advertisements, <u>you can learn a wealth of words</u> –all organized in specialized categories. Just consider, for example, what you can learn under *Pizzas*. You can find ads for the different styles of pizzas and also learn just how many different kinds of crusts <u>there are</u>. Many pizza places have <u>helpful pictures in their ads,</u> and you can also learn some interesting mottoes, such as "Fastest wheels west of the Rockies!" or "Only Chicago-style pizza in Montana!" Even if you are not living in an English-speaking country, many major libraries have telephone directories available so that you can sit down and look at the Yellow Pages for, say, Chicago or New York. Instead of throwing away those catalogs that come to your mailbox, <u>have you ever thought</u> what an excellent resource they can be for words? Because the buyer has to order sight unseen, the catalogs have excellent pictures with detailed descriptions of the products. In a large mail-order catalog, for example, you could learn <u>what a frost-free refrigerator is</u> or <u>what the names of different golf clubs are</u>. In a catalog for clothes, you could learn <u>exotic names</u> for colors and see the color itself illustrated. So, the next time you complain about not knowing enough vocabulary, get out of the house and go to the supermarket, or if you insist on staying home, pick up your telephone directory or the latest catalog <u>that came in the mail and get busy!</u>

■ Answer Key: Unit 7

EXERCISE I

___I___ 1. **Because** my sister is an accountant, she is very busy during tax time.

___I___ 2. The supermarket closes at ten; **however**, it opens at six a.m. if you need milk for breakfast.

___I___ 3. **Even though** he did not want to go to chemistry laboratory, he went anyway.

___I___ 4. Because a car is expensive, I have not bought one.

___I___ 5. Not only did Ann dislike the color of my dress, **but** she **also** did not like its style.

___I___ 6. They couldn't buy any coffee **because** the store wasn't open yet.

___I___ 7. Even though I dislike fish, I ate it at my friend's house to be polite.

___I___ 8. **Because my** mother **left the window open,** I caught a cold.

___C___ 9.

___I___ 10. I went to the bank **because** I did not have any money.

EXERCISE 2

Today's modern airport has so many services to offer travelers **that** it can resemble a city in itself. **First,** like all cities, it offers food. If you want to purchase something to eat, restaurants and snack bars abound, ranging from hot dog carts to sit-down restaurants. **However,** you might just want a little quick energy; in that event, you can buy **either** your favorite candy bar **or** a bag of chips from one of the many gift shops, which offer gifts, food, magazines, newspapers, and drugstore items. **Second,** like any city, the modern airport has entertainment. **While** waiting for your flight, you will have no problem entertaining yourself. Many airports now have a television area, **but** you could also read **or** perhaps browse among the paperbacks in the airport's bookstores. **Moreover,** some airports now have art exhibits on display. Of course, you can always entertain yourself just by watching people. **Third,** if you were unable to get all your shopping or errands done, modern airports have an array of shops and services, just like a mall in a city. **For example,** you can go to the bank or florist, buy clothes, **or** pick up last-minute gifts. Many airports in the United States now have gift shops selling products that are specialties of that state. In the Minneapolis airport, **for instance,** you can buy maple syrup and wild rice as well as Indian crafts. **Not only** do these items make thoughtful gifts **but** they also teach the tourist about the state. **Lastly,** if you want to arrive looking neat and clean **or** if you just want a pick-me-up, in many airports you can go to a unisex beauty salon. With everything that modern airports have to offer, waiting for a flight no longer needs to be boring.

so...that	subordinating	result
first	transitional	order
if	subordinating	condition
however	transitional	contrast
either...or	correlative	choice
second	transitional	order
while	subordinating	time
but	coordinating	contrast
or	coordinating	choice
moreover	transitional	addition
third	transitional	order
for example	transitional	example
or	coordinating	choice
for instance	transitional	example
not only...but also	correlative	addition
lastly	transitional	order
if	subordinating	condition
or	coordinating	choice
if	subordinating	condition

EXERCISE 3   Sample Answers:

1. Although learning English can be a long and sometimes difficult process, **it is worth the effort.**

2. Michelle has difficulty with her pronunciation; for example, **she has problems with the English "r," which is different from the French "r."**

3. Chi Fai speaks English with very little accent; however, **verb tenses are a big problem for him.**

4. Learning English is so important to Michelle and Chi Fai that **they study hard and speak English as much as possible.**

5. In addition, Michelle and Chi Fai realize that they will have to continue to practice their English to become really fluent.

EXERCISE 4

Answers will vary.

EXERCISE 5

Answers will vary.

■ Answer Key: Unit 8

EXERCISE 1

1. Credit cards **are accepted** by most restaurants.
2. The bookstore <u>must have been moved</u> since I was last here.
3. The teacher expects the assignment <u>to be done</u> by the students before the next class.
4. No change because <u>fall</u> is an intransitive verb and cannot be made passive.
5. The program <u>was interrupted</u> by the anchor for a special news bulletin.
6. By the time I get home, the mail <u>will have been delivered</u> by the letter carrier.
7. No change because the verb <u>to be</u> is intransitive.
8. Dr. Robertson's book <u>has been published</u> by the university press.
9. The dog did not like <u>being moved</u> from one house to another.
10. Although six people <u>had been expected</u> for dinner, ten showed up.

EXERCISE 2

1. We **are** constantly being asked by the government for more taxes.
2. My conversation with her **was** conducted in Vietnamese.
3. Are you sure that company still **exists?**
4. Juan has the honor of having **been** awarded the prize for the best attendance.
5. A solid friendship **was created** between them because of their common interest in soccer.
6. My fear about speaking English in public **contributed** to my shyness.
7. This English class **is offered** only to nonnative speakers.
8. When the announcement **was made** (OR **was being made**), some students were not there.
9. Some English words **are derived** (OR **have been derived**) from Latin.

EXERCISE 3

This paragraph, as written, works well, but several passive voice constructions could be changed to active without changing the focus of the paragraph which is the train. Possible changes are shown in boldface.

passive changed to active
Although our car-dependent society **has** negatively **labeled** trains as nostalgic and

many trains have long ceased to exist, a short commuter train ride can be a unique trip

                                                                         passive
into the past—and a beautiful ride. On a recent short train trip, I <u>was thrilled</u> by the

variety of bird life in the salt marsh the train passed through. In fact, the train <u>was</u>
          passive
virtually <u>ignored</u> by the stately white egrets, shiny red-winged blackbirds, and plump

mallard ducks. As we moved out of the marsh and glided along the water's edge, we
      passive
<u>were greeted</u> by the fishermen out to try their luck for the day. Farther from shore lay
                                                 passive changed to active
the oil tankers, and behind them in the distance **white sails decorated the bay.** As we

approached the city, I wondered if there was anything left **to be seen.** To my surprise, I

found myself looking into people's backyards, catching glimpses of downtown streets,
                      passive
and, best of all, <u>being treated</u> to a panoramic view of the highway. There cars were

creeping along, bumper to bumper, while out on the tracks, we peacefully glided by,

rocking gently on the rails. I like to think that as our whistle tooted, a driver out
  passive changed to active
there **may have heard** it who wished he or she were on the train.

■ Answer Key: Unit 9

EXERCISE

Sample Answers:

   There are many differences between third-world and industrialized nations. One important difference is in the types of worries individuals have in their daily lives. All humans have worries but what one group of people may worry about can be of little importance to another group of people. In many parts of the world, people never think about buying new clothes or the latest model TV set or car. All that they think about is how they can get food and be free from hunger. Such a fear frightens these people and causes them enormous worry. In contrast, people who live in wealthy nations usually never think about food except where or when they are going to eat, but they have different problems in their lives, such as too much work, family problems, and stress. In both types of countries, rich and poor, people are never free from worry.

■ Answer Key: Unit 10

EXERCISE 1

  I   1. Marta's children **are** certainly well-behaved.

  C   2.

  I   3. Matthew, who is in second grade, already **knows** how to read and write.

  C   4.

  I   5. If a child in China **performs** well enough in his or her sport, the child will have a chance to receive professional training.

  I   6. Parents usually **want** the best for their children.

  I   7. Brainstorming **helps** a writer to gather ideas and avoid writer's block.

  I   8. There **are** several stages in the writing process, including prewriting, writing a draft, and revising.

  I   9. Because of the drought, there is not enough water for all the farmers who need it.

EXERCISE 2

differs (differ)
is (be)
are (be)
find (find)
have (have)
walks (walk)
has (have)
helps (help)
is (be)
answers (answer)
have (have)
has (have)

EXERCISE 3

April 15 is a well-known date in the United States. Every year on this day, everyone who **works** must file his or her income tax forms with both the federal and state governments. Filing these forms is no easy task. First, a person needs to decide which forms to file. For federal income taxes, there is a long form for people who **wish** to itemize their deductions. This form **has** at least five supplementary parts, called "schedules," and a person must decide which of these, if any, to file as well. Then there is a short form for people who **plan** to take the "standard" deduction, one that **has** been precalculated and is the same for everyone. The state income-tax forms are separate forms, and these must also be filed. In California, there **are** at least four supplementary schedules that a person may need to fill out. Once a person **knows** which ones to file, completing all of these forms is not easy either, and many people **hire** an accountant to help them. Regardless of whether a taxpayer **chooses** to complete the forms on his or her own or to seek assistance, the forms must be postmarked before midnight on April 15. This day is one of the busiest for the U.S. Postal Service since many taxpayers find themselves finishing the whole process at the last minute.

■ Answer Key: Unit 11

EXERCISE I

<u> I </u> 1. At the end of each quarter, final exams are held.

<u> I </u> 2. Most of **the** students in Chemistry 1 have to study very hard.

<u> C </u> 3.

<u> I </u> 4. If students ride their bikes to school, they need to make sure that **the** brakes on their bicycles are working.

<u> I </u> 5. At night, all patrons must wear shirts and ties in this restaurant.

<u> I </u> 6. One of **the** best recent inventions has been the computer.

<u> I </u> 7. If I have problems with my car, I take **the** bus to work.

<u> I </u> 8. Be sure that you study **the** night before **the** (OR **an**) exam.

<u> C </u> 9.

<u> I </u> 10. When there is **a** full moon, I like to go for a walk down Beach Avenue.

<u> I </u> 11. In California, water is a precious commodity when there is a drought.

<u> I </u> 12. Although I like to write down my thoughts, I never have enough time to write in **my** (OR **a**) journal.

EXERCISE 2

    My parents taught me to love <u>learning</u> when I was still very young. Every evening after <u>dinner</u>, my father would teach me <u>simple math</u> and my mother would teach me how to write and read <u>Chinese characters</u>. At the age of five, I already knew a number of Chinese characters and was able to do addition, <u>subtraction</u>, and <u>simple multiplication problems</u>. It wasn't that I was <u>a genius</u> or even a precocious child; it was <u>the simple fact</u> that my parents encouraged me to learn by praising me whenever I gave them <u>the correct answer</u> to their questions. Their praise made me feel that I was smart and could learn. What also helped me learn was that I had <u>few distractions</u>. I did not grow up with <u>a television</u>, a radio, or <u>video games</u> as children do now, for it was not common in <u>China</u> at that time to have a television or a radio at home. Therefore, our usual source of entertainment after dinner was <u>playing games</u>, <u>reading</u>, and learning. When I began school, I never had to depend on <u>the teacher</u> to motivate me to learn because I had already developed a love of learning. I also entered <u>school</u> with the attitude that I could learn because my parents' early teaching and <u>the learning</u> that had taken place in my house had helped me develop not only <u>confidence</u> in my abilities but also <u>a sense</u> that learning was enjoyable.

learning	uncountable	not identified
dinner	set expression	
simple math	uncountable	not identified
Chinese characters	plural	not identified
subtraction	uncountable	not identified
simple multiplication problems	plural	not identified
a genius	singular, countable	not identified
the simple fact	post-modification	identified

the correct answer	shared knowledge	identified
few distractions	plural	not identified
a television	singular, countable	not identified
video games	plural	not identified
China	name of a place	
playing games	uncountable	not identified
reading	uncountable	not identified
the teacher	shared knowledge	identified
school	uncountable	not identified
the learning	post-modification	identified
confidence	uncountable	not identified
a sense	singular, countable	not identified

EXERCISE 3

My attitude toward English is negatively affecting my writing. I think the problem is that as a mathematics major, I love to spend my time doing as much math as possible. Often my math homework and my other classes, which also relate to my major, occupy most of my time. As a result, I devote the rest of my time and energy, which is not much, to writing essays for my English class. However, I usually have trouble getting started. I waste my time eating, listening to music, or even looking in the mirror instead of trying to work on my paper. Furthermore, I always have a negative feeling toward writing. Even before writing a paper, I assume that my paper will not turn out well. Because of this negative attitude, my grade in English is suffering.

EXERCISE 4

Answers will vary.

■ Answer Key: Unit 12

EXERCISE I

1. When I read, I mark unfamiliar **vocabulary**, which I later look up a dictionary.
2. This **boy** needs (OR **These boys need**) to sign up for the camping trip.
3. One of the best **ways** to practice your English is to join a conversation club.
4. Many cultures teach respect for the **elderly**.
5. I had three **pieces of candy** and some cake at the party.
6. My writing needs **improvement**, so I am going to work with a tutor.
7. My friends are renting a **hundred**-year-old house.
8. The professor is hiring students to analyze the **data** she collected.
9. You need to follow the laboratory manual **step by step** to make your experiment come out right.
10. I had almost given up finding my watch when it suddenly caught my **eye** from under a piece of paper.

11. My aunt has five **children**: two sons and three **daughters**.
12. My roommate has excellent **computer** skills.

EXERCISE 2

During the fall quarter, I was overwhelmed with many **assignments**. The most unexpected one was writing. Even though I knew that education **classes** required writing, the professors I had were especially fond of essay writing. Both of my education **classes** required a total of eight **papers**, each of which were four to six **pages** long; in addition, the final papers in both classes were twenty-page research papers. Furthermore, both of my biochemistry **classes** required a total of eight lab write-ups and three essays. In sum, I had to write more than twenty papers last quarter; and **those** papers were a nightmare for me. Previously, I thought that only English classes would require a lot of writing which is not one of my favorite **activities**. Nevertheless, last semester was the only time during my four years in college that I had to write so much. Thus, I lost much of my fear of writing; however, I still hate revision because it is very time-consuming work.

EXERCISE 3

Catalog shopping has become very popular in the United **States**. According to a recent newspaper article, catalog sales have been growing at the rate of 15 percent annually, twice the growth rate of retail store sales. With the **advent** of 800 **numbers** and fax machines, catalog shopping has indeed become fast and convenient. You can telephone in your order, speak to the salesperson at the other end, and usually find out if what you want is in stock, thus avoiding the tedious **work** of filling out an order form. Or, if you prefer a written record, you can use the order form provided in the catalog and fax it to the catalog company. These days, it is possible to buy everything from a simple white blouse to a whole set of garden **furniture** without ever setting foot in a store. Most people also like the option of express mail that **catalog** companies offer; customers can send an order one day and the item will arrive at their house a day or two after. People also find that if they purchase **clothing** from the same catalog companies, they can avoid much **frustration**, for they can almost always gauge the right size. Also, catalogs help by showing a picture of the range of colors. However, what the catalogs do not mention is that while you can return your purchase, it is time-consuming to repack and send it. Thus, if you get what you wanted, you have saved time. However, if you are disappointed, you will have to devote time to repackaging and returning the item. If you are too busy or lazy to do so and thus keep the unwanted item, you will lose money. However, a wonderful **alternative** is the catalog store. You can see what you want in the catalog and then go to the catalog store and buy it. Then you have the best of both **worlds**.

EXERCISE 4

Answers will vary.

EXERCISE 5

Answers will vary.

■ Answer Key: Unit 13

EXERCISE 1

A. Word-choice errors with words other than prepositions

1. Arturo called to say he would be late; in the **meantime**, I read a book.
2. Apartments are so expensive that his family has to **cram** into a two-room apartment.
3. Her excellence in teaching has earned her **awards** (OR **recognition**).
4. I once was in a math class where everyone was motivated to **achieve** the best test score.
5. When Samir cannot answer in class, he feels **small**.
6. Jennifer's bad grade on her final exam in French **kept** her from passing the course.
7. I became so **curious** that I decided to investigate the noise.
8. Students are also **doing** their part in keeping the school clean by not littering.
9. During the first few months of school, I was **speechless** both in class and at lunchtime because of my inability to speak English.
10. After she had been studying English for six weeks, Madeleine expected to know everything, but **instead** she found she had just begun.

B. Word-choice errors with prepositions

1. They had to be nice **to** their neighbors.
2. My brother is a student **at** Harvard University, and I am a student **in** the music department **at** the University of Michigan.
3. The revised schedule gives students a choice **of** dates and times.
4. All the graduate classes in the education department are held **in** the early afternoon and evening.
5. It's easy to clean the kitchen when all you do is load dishes **into** the dishwasher.
6. My lab partner lives **at** 1003 Rosemont Avenue.
7. Living in an apartment is difficult if you are not happy **with** your roommates.
8. If you are hunting for your car keys, I saw them lying **on** the table.
9. If my trip goes as planned, I will see you **on** Monday.
10. My uncle, who owns a successful business, has had a big influence **on** me.

EXERCISE 2

When I was a senior in high school, I dreamed about being a college student and often wondered what the college would **be like**. I also wondered about how much difference there would be between college and high school, particularly in class size. I **attended** (OR **went to**) a big-city high school, which was crowded; each class had an enrollment of 40 students. Therefore, when I sent in my application for college, I hoped that classes in college would be small. However, here at college, especially for chemistry and economics classes, the **lecture halls** (OR **classrooms**) are overcrowded. For instance, my chemistry class has more than 300 **students** in it and some of them cannot get a seat when they come late. Some students stand **by** the back door and others sit **in** the **aisles**. Unfortunately, when a class is very crowded, I cannot focus on what the teacher is saying and I do not feel I am learning. My hope that classes would be small in college has been destroyed. (OR My expectation that classes would be small in college has not been realized.)

EXERCISE 3

Answers will vary.

EXERCISE 4

Answers will vary.

■ Answer Key: Unit 14

Common Word Suffixes

Sample Answers:

Noun Suffixes

–ment	requirement
–ness	happiness
–tion	examination
–sion	discussion
–ity	maturity
–ence	confidence
–ance	resistance
–ure	fixture
–er	painter
–ism	racism
–ist	economist
–ship	relationship

Verb Suffixes

–ate	originate
–en	lighten
–ify	testify
–ize	organize

Adjective Suffixes

–ous	precious
–ful	hopeful
–less	hopeless
–ive	informative
–able	washable

Adjective Suffixes *(continued)*

–ent	confident
–ant	resistant
–ic	economic
–al	informal
–some	tiresome
–ate	moderate
–y	cloudy
–ly	lovely
–like	lifelike
–an	Korean
–ese	Chinese
–ing	surprising
–ed	surprised

Adverb Suffix

–ly	quickly

EXERCISE I

	Noun	Verb	Adjective	Adverb
1.	characteristic	characterize	characteristic	characteristically
2.	approximation	approximate	approximate	approximately
3.	prediction	predict	predictable	predictably
4.	dependence	depend	dependent	dependently
5.	production	produce	productive	productively
6.	origin	originate	original	originally
7.	sufficiency	suffice	sufficient	sufficiently
8.	emphasis	emphasize	emphatic	emphatically
9.	specification	specify	specific	specifically
10.	significance	signify	significant	significantly

EXERCISE 2

__I__   1. Writing under the pressure of time gives us several **benefits** including the ability to think fast and to organize fast.

__C__   2.

__I__   3. Many immigrants become **mature** by dealing with adult problems at an early age.

__I__   4. China is located in **central** Asia.

__I__   5. I don't see why a young child should be punished **harshly**.

__I__   6. Ora came to the United States to **pursue** her Ph.D.

__I__   7. In order to **succeed,** one must be able to make sacrifices.

__C__   8.

__I__   9. My **suggestion** is aimed at easing the problem.

__I__ 10. If I keep writing in this fashion, my writing skills might even become **worse,**
for I might get used to making those mistakes.

__I__ 11. When my husband cooks, I have to clean up the **mess** he makes.

__C__ 12.

EXERCISE 3

1. **excited** (excite)
2. **surprising** (surprise)
3. **depressing** (depress)
4. **interested** (interest)
5. **puzzled** (puzzle)
6. **amazing** (amaze)
7. **depressed** (depress)
8. **astonishing** (astonish)
9. **surprised** (surprise)
10. **entertaining** (entertain)

EXERCISE 4

My bilingualism may benefit me in terms of job opportunities. First of all, more and more **immigrants** arrive in the United States every year. To help these new **immigrants** or to do business with them, bilingual and multilingual employees are needed. For example, banks, law firms, and insurance agencies often need employees who can **communicate** with both non-English speakers and English-speaking clients. Therefore, because I speak Spanish **well,** I might find many job opportunities in places where there are a lot of Spanish speakers, such as Los Angeles, New York, Chicago, and Miami. Secondly, if I can **achieve** my goal of having my own **dental** clinic, Spanish-speaking clients may be a good source for my **earnings.** Many Spanish speakers **tend** to feel more **comfortable** with Spanish-speaking doctors and dentists. Even Mexicans and Mexican-Americans who speak English very well often still **prefer** to go to Spanish-speaking dentists instead of English-speaking dentists. So, overall, I may benefit **economically** from my **knowledge** of two languages.

EXERCISE 5

Being multilingual enables me to communicate **directly** with many people. Even though I mostly use English in my everyday life, especially at the university, I still use Cantonese to communicate with my relatives. My grandmother, for example, who just recently came to the United States from Vietnam and is now living with my family, cannot understand English. The only language she speaks **fluently** is Cantonese. Therefore, knowing how to speak Cantonese allows me to communicate **easily** with her. By talking with her, I have learned some of my family's **history.** She told me that she and my grandfather were originally from China and she **explained** what her life was like there. She has also told me **interesting** stories about China that I never would have heard if I could not speak Cantonese. Moreover, being able to speak Cantonese or Vietnamese in Chinese and Vietnamese restaurants has also been **beneficial** to me. The restaurant employees recognize that they and I are from similar backgrounds because we speak the same language. They, therefore, give more **attention** to me than to customers who do not speak the language. Thus, being able to speak these languages opens the door for me to **communicate** closely with many different people.

EXERCISE 6

Answers will vary.

■ Answer Key: Unit 15

EXERCISE

1. My mother did not let us go to the mall alone **when we were little (very young, small)**.
2. By talking to native speakers, I can **learn a little about American customs**.
3. According to an essay in **the May 20th issue of** *Time,* job openings for college graduates dropped ten percent in the 1990–91 academic year.
4. That red blouse doesn't **go with those purple jeans**.
5. My aunt, who lives in Los Angeles, takes the bus everywhere because she is afraid to drive **on the freeway**.
6. Now that my English has improved, I can **communicate with my friends**.
7. After talking with my teacher, I **understand the lecture better**.
8. It was blowing very hard and then the wind died down **all of a sudden**.

INDEX